THE CHESS

PLAYER'S BIBLE

2nd Edition

THE CHESS

PLAYER'S BIBLE

2nd Edition

**Illustrated Strategies for
Staying Ahead of the Game**

**James Eade
Al Lawrence**

THE CHESS PLAYER'S BIBLE
A QUARTO BOOK

Second edition for the United States, its territories and dependencies, and Canada published in 2023 by Sourcebooks.
Previous edition for the United States, its territories and dependencies, and Canada published in 2004 by Barron's Educational Series, Inc.

All inquiries should be addressed to:
Sourcebooks Inc.
P.O. Box 4410, Naperville
Illinois 60567-4410
(630) 961-3900
www.sourcebooks.com

ISBN: 978-1-4380-8942-3

Library of Congress Control No. 2014951300

QUAR.CPB2

Conceived, edited, and designed by
Quarto Publishing
an imprint of The Quarto Group
1 Triptych Place
London SE1 9SH

Senior Editors Katie Crous, Liz Pasfield
Art Director Caroline Guest
Senior Art Editor Penny Cobb
Copy Editor Ian Kingston
Designers Elizabeth Healey, Tania Field
Photographer Paul Forrester
Illustrators Carol Woodcock, John Woodcock
Proofreaders Claire Waite Brown, Sue Viccars
Indexer Diana LeCore

Creative Director Moira Clinch
Publisher Paul Carslake

Printed in China

9 8 7 6 5 4 3 2

Contents

INTRODUCTION

The Chess Player's Bible is an illustrated guide to chess concepts and terminology. It is designed to appeal to someone who may never have considered purchasing a book on chess before, even though they enjoy playing the game. It includes everything you need to know in order to play the game and win.

More books have been written about chess than any other game. One may legitimately wonder why we need another. Well, most chess books are highly technical, and are written for the serious student of the game. The vast majority of chess players are unlikely to use such books.

Even books targeting beginners often start with chess notation and immediately assume fluency on the part of the reader. That approach makes life easier for the author, but it can also be discouraging for the novice or casual player. *The Chess Player's Bible* makes use of notation to some extent, but

certainly does not rely on it.

This book's approach is more visually oriented than most. Concepts and terms are represented pictorially, and graphics are used to draw the reader's attention to key elements of what I'm trying to convey. If you have read this far, you've already read more text than you will encounter on any other page in the book.

Most of us are taught to play chess by someone else, usually a parent or other relative. We generally assume that they know what they're talking about, but that isn't always the case. There are many chess players playing and

enjoying a game that is very much like chess, but with certain oddities attributable to nothing more than local folklore.

The "Getting Started" section covers all of the essential knowledge about how the pieces move, what constitutes check and checkmate, and the special rules that may not be universally understood. It's certainly possible to enjoy a game without knowing all the rules (or there wouldn't be so many weekend golfers!), but I believe that the enjoyment can only be enhanced by playing the game properly.

What's In A Name? Chess terminology is used and abused even more often than the rules. It can be a rather arcane subject that stumps even veteran players. One year I was lounging poolside between rounds at the annual U.S. Open. I struck up a conversation with another tournament participant. After an exchange of pleasantries, I confessed that I was having difficulty defending against 1 e4. (Don't worry, if you don't know what that means.) He promptly advised me to use the King's Indian Defense (KID), which is all well and good, except that the KID is used against 1 d4, not 1 e4.

If a long-time tournament veteran can get his terminology mixed up, it can happen to almost anyone. A glossary of terms is generally included in order to keep things straight, but it is my experience that people often need more in the way of guidance than a mere definition of terms. This book

defines chess terminology, and illustrates it as well.

You can enjoy a game of chess if you call a rook a castle, or a knight a horse, but in some circles you're going to call the kind of attention to yourself that you do not want. Chess has a long history and a distinctive culture and it never hurts to appreciate it.

Chess is truly an international game, and this can create havoc when it comes to chess naming conventions. The section on "Game Types" includes the names of chess openings as they are used in the United States. Just be aware that the opening called the *Ruy Lopez* in the United States is called the *Spanish* in Europe, and that there are many such discrepancies.

Inside The Book Although many openings are covered in these pages, it is by no means definitive. Even a standard opening reference such as *Modern Chess Openings*, by Grandmaster Nick de Firmian, cannot be considered comprehensive. There are simply too many chess variations to present in a single volume, and new ones are being introduced every year.

The moves that define each of the most common chess openings are illustrated along with a representative continuation. Just keep in mind that chess variations branch out so quickly that it is impossible to cover them all.

One of the mysteries of chess that captures the imagination is how certain set patterns continue to surface despite the fact that games can take such radically different courses. The section on "Mating Patterns" will help you to identify some of the most common ones. Once you learn to recognize them, you may be surprised at how frequently these possibilities appear in your own games.

Tactics are another recurring pattern in chess. A tactic called the *pin*, for instance, occurs in nearly every game. The key to this type of pattern recognition is repetition.

The way pawns are arranged in a chess game is of critical importance. Pattern recognition plays an important role here too. The section on "Pawns" covers some of the most frequently occurring setups, and will help guide your play.

The last part of the book is dedicated to the final phase of the game: the endgame. Fewer pieces do not always translate into easier games! This phase is deceptively subtle and difficult to master. However, an understanding of the endgame will pay huge dividends in terms of your overall understanding of the entire game. Even early opening moves can have consequences that play out in an ending.

In this revised edition, edited by Al Lawrence, Mastery Challenges have been introduced at the end of each section in which you can test knowledge gained from the preceding pages and prepare for skills yet to be learned. There is also a quick-reference "How to Win Chess Games" article, for immediate improvement, and a Game Analysis section that takes you through momentous chess games, following the moves of the game's most influential players.

There is no need to read this book sequentially, because the sections are generally independent of one another. If you are new to the game, then by all means spend time in the "Getting Started" section; otherwise, just skip ahead to any topic that takes your interest. Most importantly, keep in mind what some serious tournament players often forget: chess is meant to be enjoyed. Have fun!

JAMES EADE

How To Use This Book

Chess concepts are represented pictorially in this book and the basic methods are described below. The "Getting Started" section on p.10 and Key on p.283 also provide information on the symbols used and chess notation.

The Chessboards

Red arrow An attack (direct or indirect) on the opponent's piece or pieces.

Ghosting Represents a move by a piece from one square to another.

Red grouping Referring to more than one piece.

Highlighting Draws attention to a described square, or squares. Yellow highlighting is used if needed to differentiate from red. Highlighting can also represent squares which a piece is controlling.

Chess Notation

× Indicates a capture.

+ Check.

Checkmate.

0-0 Castling short (on the kingside).

0-0-0 Castling long (on the queenside).

... Indicates that the next move is by black.

e.p. En passant.

The Pieces

☗ or K: King

♛ or Q: Queen

♖ or R: Rook

♘ or N: Knight

If no symbol is given before a move, it is a pawn move.

♗ or B: Bishop

Section 1: GETTING STARTED

Everyone can teach themselves to play chess by patiently studying the rules of the game. Read through this section carefully and get to grips with the basics before you start to play.

The Chessboard

A chessboard may look empty if there are no pieces on it, but it is still filled with information. The board is divided into files (columns), ranks (rows), and diagonals. Each square has a unique name, which is defined by its file and rank. These coordinates are shown around the edges of the diagram.

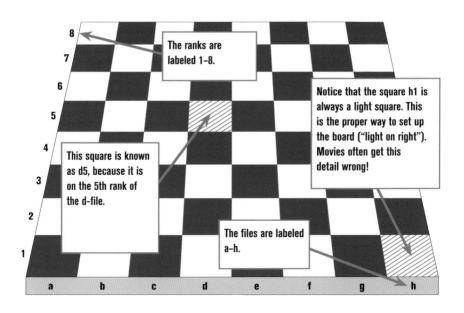

The ranks are labeled 1–8.

Notice that the square h1 is always a light square. This is the proper way to set up the board ("light on right"). Movies often get this detail wrong!

This square is known as d5, because it is on the 5th rank of the d-file.

The files are labeled a–h.

Diagonals Although only files and ranks are used to identify squares, diagonals are also an important part of the chessboard. If it weren't for the diagonals, bishops wouldn't be able to move at all!

The diagonals are identified from their lowest rank to their highest. This is referred to as the a1–h8 diagonal.

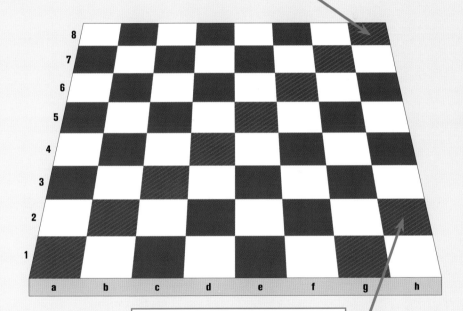

This is one of the shortest diagonals and is referred to as g1–h2. Usually, the most important diagonals are the ones that cross the center of the board. They're the longest ones, and that is usually where the action takes place in a chess game.

The Pieces

Different pieces have different powers. Learning how to coordinate their movements effectively is one of the game's primary challenges. A few starting tips: White moves first, and then white and black take turns making one move at a time. No "passes" are allowed! In this book, we use both letters and symbols for the pieces.

The King The king is a slow-moving piece, but it is the most valuable one. If your king is lost, so is the game. The king may move one square in any direction. ☛ See also Check Versus Checkmate p.18, and Castling p.33.

The king may move to any of the highlighted squares. If it were to move to the e5 square, it would be written down as Ke5. A capital K or ♔ is used to symbolize the king.

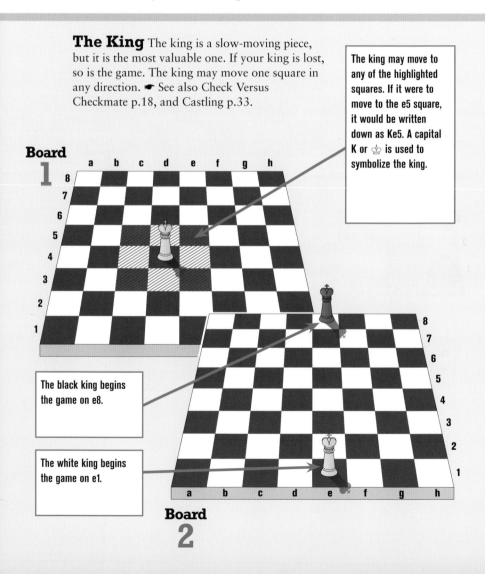

Board 1

The black king begins the game on e8.

The white king begins the game on e1.

Board 2

The Rook

The Rook The rook is a powerful piece, which is outranked only by the queen. It may move any number of unoccupied squares both horizontally and vertically. ☛ See also Castling p.33.

The rook may move anywhere along the d-file.

The rook may move anywhere along the 4th rank.

Rooks cannot move diagonally. Even though the king could move to e5 from d4 in one move, the rook would need two. For example, you could play ① ♖ e4 and ② ♖ e5. A capital R is used to symbolize the rook when writing moves or the symbol ♖ is used.

The rooks begin the game in the board's corners.

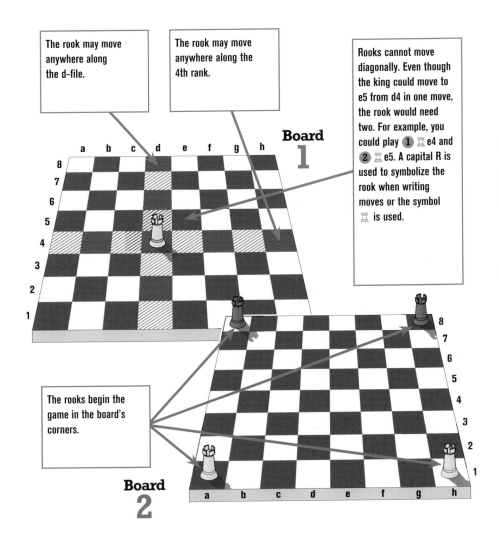

Board 1

Board 2

The Bishop The bishop is not as strong a piece as the rook. It covers almost as much ground as the rook if it is in the middle of the board, but loses strength as it moves away from the center. The bishop is confined to the diagonals and cannot move horizontally or vertically. Also, it must always remain on the same color square as the one it starts from.

The a8 square is on a different color square from the one the bishop occupies on d4. Therefore, the bishop can never move here. A capital B is used to symbolize the bishop and the symbol ♗ is used when printing a bishop move.

The bishop may move anywhere along the g1–a7 diagonal.

The bishop can move anywhere along the a1–h8 diagonal.

This is how the bishops are positioned at the start of the game.

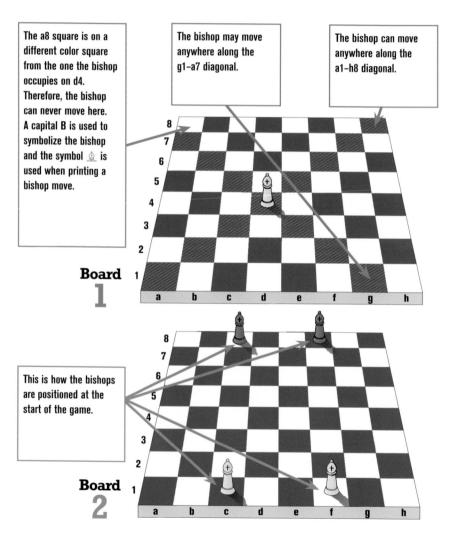

Board 1

Board 2

The Queen The queen is the most powerful piece in chess and combines the movements of the rook and bishop. She can move any number of unoccupied squares vertically, horizontally, or diagonally. The queen is too valuable to be given up lightly. She needs to be protected from capture. Losing your queen does not lose the game, but it greatly reduces your fighting capacity.

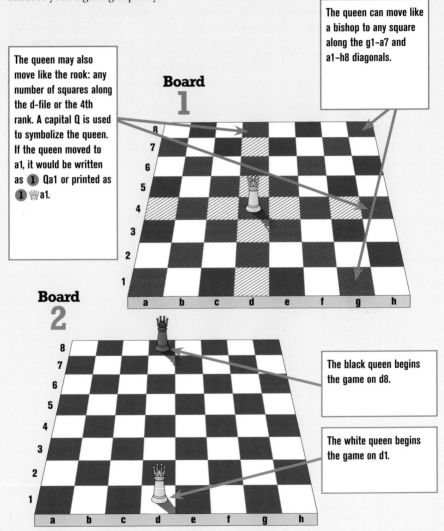

The queen can move like a bishop to any square along the g1–a7 and a1–h8 diagonals.

The queen may also move like the rook: any number of squares along the d-file or the 4th rank. A capital Q is used to symbolize the queen. If the queen moved to a1, it would be written as **1** Qa1 or printed as **1** ♕a1.

Board 1

Board 2

The black queen begins the game on d8.

The white queen begins the game on d1.

The Knight The knight's move is the most difficult one to explain. A one–two approach is usually used, which means that if the knight moves one square horizontally, it must move two squares vertically. Alternatively, if the knight moves one square vertically, it must then move two squares horizontally. As long as the destination square is unoccupied, the knight can move to it. The knight is the only piece capable of jumping over others.

Color also matters to the knight. It oscillates or alternates between colors. If it is on a light square it may only move to a dark square, and vice versa.

The knight is on a dark square on d4 and may move only to the highlighted light squares. One of the possible moves would be **1** ♞ e6. We use a capital N to symbolize the knight when writing moves, because K is already being used to denote the king.

Board 1

This is how the knights are positioned at the beginning of the game.

Board 2

The Pawn The pawn is the basic unit of force in chess. It is the least powerful piece, but it is unique in several ways. It is the only piece that cannot move backward. It may move either one or two squares forward on its first turn, but afterward it can move only one square at a time. It also captures in a different way than it normally moves. No other piece can make that claim.

A pawn can move forward if there is no piece on the square immediately in front of it, but it captures enemy pieces diagonally. ☛ See also En Passant p.31 and Promotion p.32.

> If it is white's turn to play, the pawn could move to f5 or capture the black pawn on g5. When writing moves, if we give only the square designations it is assumed to be a pawn move. So, if white played the pawn on f4 to f5, it would be written ① f5. The capture would be written ① f×g5, where the × indicates that a capture has taken place.

Board
1

> Neither the pawn on d4 nor the one on d5 can move.

Board
2

> This is the position of all the pieces at the beginning of a chess game. Notice that the h1 square is always a light square.

Check Versus Checkmate

Check is not the same as checkmate. Many beginners give check whenever they can, but experienced players know that checks may sometimes backfire on you. Checkmate never does.

Check A check is an attack on the enemy king. If an enemy piece is attacking your king, you are in check. A check may not be ignored: you must immediately get out of check. There are three different ways of dealing with a check. You may (1) capture the attacking piece; (2) move a different piece between the king and the attacker; or (3) move the king to a safe square. The symbol + is used to represent a check in chess notation.

Checkmate If your king is in check and you cannot escape it by any of the methods shown above, you are in checkmate. Checkmate means that the game is over. The checkmated player loses. The symbol # is used to represent a checkmate in chess notation.

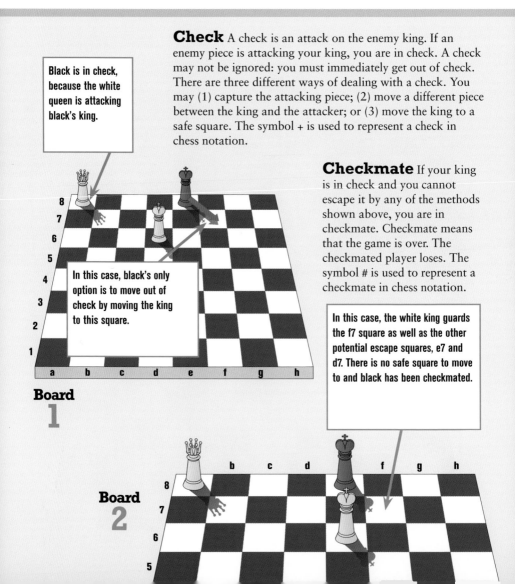

Black is in check, because the white queen is attacking black's king.

In this case, black's only option is to move out of check by moving the king to this square.

In this case, the white king guards the f7 square as well as the other potential escape squares, e7 and d7. There is no safe square to move to and black has been checkmated.

Board 1

Board 2

Draw A draw is a completed chess game without a winner. A game may end in a draw by a variety of ways, but the most common is a mutual agreement by the players. A stalemate is also a draw (☛ see Stalemate Versus Checkmate p.20). In tournament play there are additional rules that can result in a draw. If the same position is repeated three times (not necessarily in a row) with the same player to move and all possible moves the same, either player may claim a draw. If fifty moves go by without a capture or any pawn move, either player may claim a draw. You may also declare a draw if your opponent has insufficient checkmating material (a king and knight alone, for example, cannot checkmate a lone king).

Black's only defense is to continually check the white king. The king cannot escape these checks and the result is a draw by what's referred to as *perpetual check.*

White is threatening checkmate by playing the queen to g7.

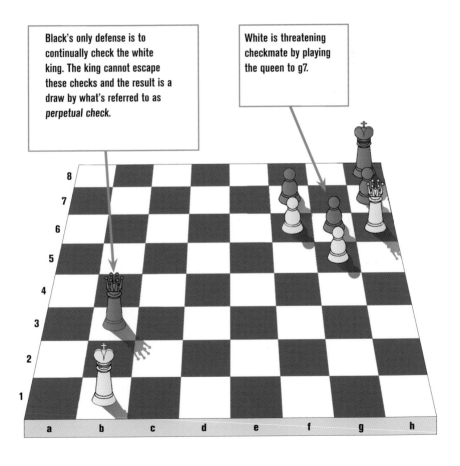

Stalemate Versus Checkmate

Checkmate (sometimes shortened to "mate") is the ultimate conclusion to a game of chess, and wins the game. If your opponent has no legal move and is not in check, then you have stalemate, not checkmate. A stalemate is only a draw. In tournaments, the winner of a game is given one point and the loser zero. A draw awards each player a half point.

Stalemate The best way to guard against stalemate in a king and queen versus king situation is to pin the king down to the edge of the board, but to do it from a distance.

The queen attacks all the squares that the black king could move to, but is not checking the king. If it is black's turn to play, the result is stalemate. White has squandered his winning advantage!

Checkmate with queen and king: Now the black king is trapped on the 8th rank, and there is no danger of falling into a stalemate.

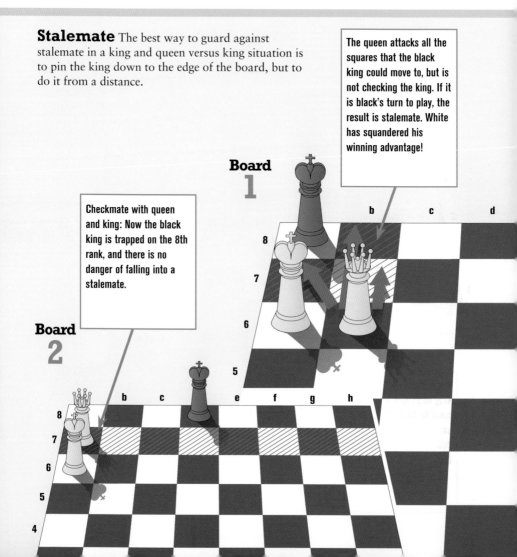

Now, the idea is to simply march the white king along the 6th
rank until it approaches the black king.

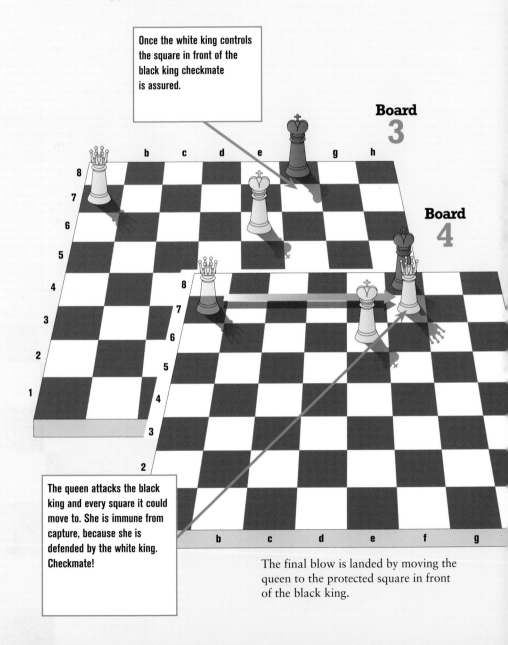

Once the white king controls
the square in front of the
black king checkmate
is assured.

Board
3

Board
4

The queen attacks the black
king and every square it could
move to. She is immune from
capture, because she is
defended by the white king.
Checkmate!

The final blow is landed by moving the
queen to the protected square in front
of the black king.

King and Two Rooks Versus King
Two rooks can deliver mate without any help from the king.

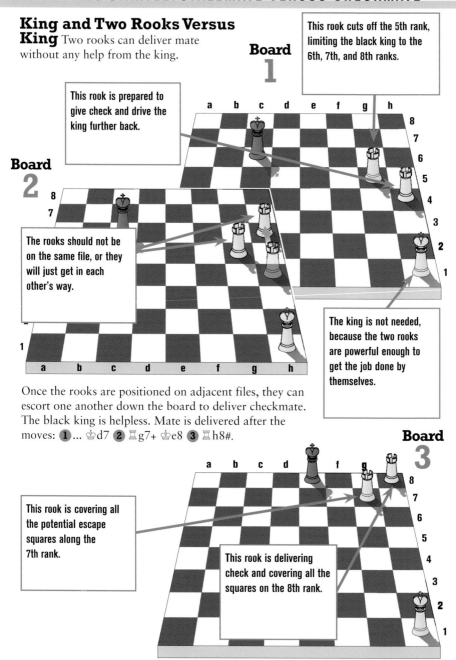

This rook cuts off the 5th rank, limiting the black king to the 6th, 7th, and 8th ranks.

Board 1

This rook is prepared to give check and drive the king further back.

Board 2

The rooks should not be on the same file, or they will just get in each other's way.

The king is not needed, because the two rooks are powerful enough to get the job done by themselves.

Once the rooks are positioned on adjacent files, they can escort one another down the board to deliver checkmate. The black king is helpless. Mate is delivered after the moves: **1** ... ♚d7 **2** ♖g7+ ♚e8 **3** ♖h8#.

Board 3

This rook is covering all the potential escape squares along the 7th rank.

This rook is delivering check and covering all the squares on the 8th rank.

King and Two Bishops Versus King

Two bishops are not as powerful as two rooks. They need support from the king in order to deliver checkmate. However, they are powerful enough to restrict the enemy king to one area of the board quite easily. The winning method is to keep shrinking the area of the board available to the king until it is ultimately trapped in a corner and mated.

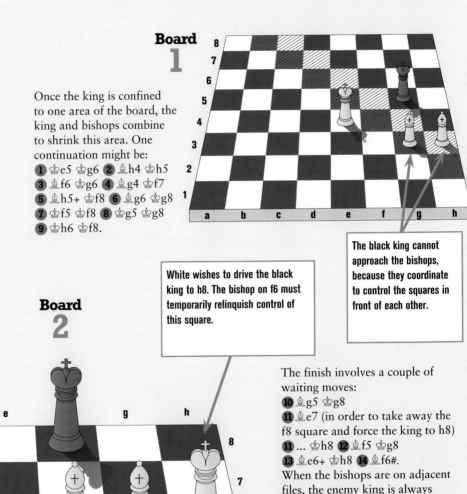

Board 1

Once the king is confined to one area of the board, the king and bishops combine to shrink this area. One continuation might be:

1 ♔e5 ♚g6 2 ♗h4 ♚h5
3 ♗f6 ♚g6 4 ♗g4 ♚f7
5 ♗h5+ ♚f8 6 ♗g6 ♚g8
7 ♔f5 ♚f8 8 ♔g5 ♚g8
9 ♔h6 ♚f8.

The black king cannot approach the bishops, because they coordinate to control the squares in front of each other.

White wishes to drive the black king to h8. The bishop on f6 must temporarily relinquish control of this square.

Board 2

The finish involves a couple of waiting moves:

10 ♗g5 ♚g8
11 ♗e7 (in order to take away the f8 square and force the king to h8)
11 ... ♚h8 12 ♗f5 ♚g8
13 ♗e6+ ♚h8 14 ♗f6#.

When the bishops are on adjacent files, the enemy king is always trapped in one area of the board. Systematically shrink the available area, and then force the king into a corner. The lone king is defenseless.

King and Rook Versus King A king and rook can always checkmate a lone king. They must work together to drive the king to the edge of the board. The main idea is to keep cutting off squares so that the king has fewer and fewer options until it finally must move to the edge of the board. Check is not checkmate, and you should only give a check if it is consistent with the idea of cutting off squares.

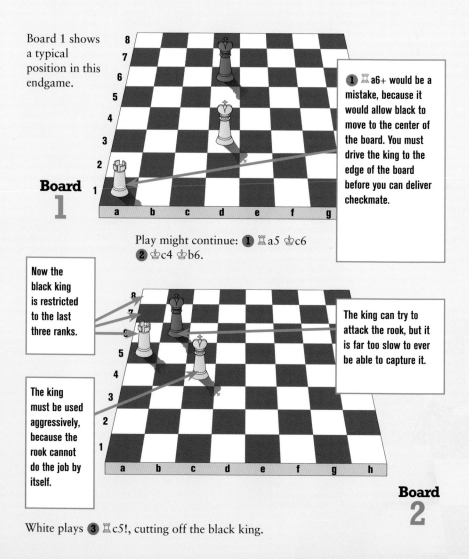

Board 1 shows a typical position in this endgame.

Board 1

1 ♖a6+ would be a mistake, because it would allow black to move to the center of the board. You must drive the king to the edge of the board before you can deliver checkmate.

Play might continue: 1 ♖a5 ♔c6 2 ♔c4 ♔b6.

Now the black king is restricted to the last three ranks.

The king can try to attack the rook, but it is far too slow to ever be able to capture it.

The king must be used aggressively, because the rook cannot do the job by itself.

Board 2

White plays 3 ♖c5!, cutting off the black king.

The rook and king continue to work together in order to
drive the black king into a corner of the board. You must
be willing to waste a move in certain circumstances in
order to make further progress.

White cannot improve
the position of the king
or rook. Moving the
rook along the 7th rank
would allow black to
escape via c8. White
must waste a move
with the rook along the
c-file in order to force
black to the corner of
the board.

Board 3

This position could arise after a few more moves:
3 … ♚b7 **4** ♔b5 ♚a7 **5** ♖c7+ ♚a8 **6** ♔b6 ♚b8.

Any first move
backward along the
c-file by the rook
would suffice. Black
has no choice but to
play **7** … ♚a8,
which allows
8 ♖c8#.

The game ends:
7 ♖c6 ♚a8 **8** ♖c8#.

The king is needed in
order to prevent the
king's escape via the
7th rank once the rook
gives check along
the 8th.

Board 4

Bishop, Knight, and King Versus King The most complicated mate is the one with just a bishop and knight. The two pieces don't coordinate very well. In this case it isn't enough to simply drive the king to the edge of the board, or even to any one of the corners. It must be driven into the same color corner as the bishop. If you have a light-squared bishop, you must drive the king into a light square corner.

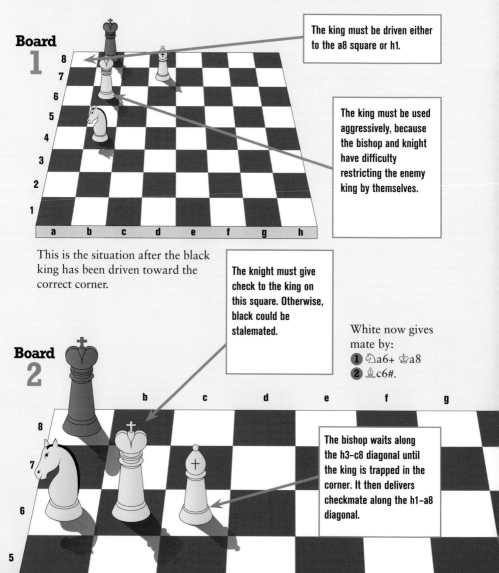

Board 1

> The king must be driven either to the a8 square or h1.

> The king must be used aggressively, because the bishop and knight have difficulty restricting the enemy king by themselves.

This is the situation after the black king has been driven toward the correct corner.

> The knight must give check to the king on this square. Otherwise, black could be stalemated.

White now gives mate by:
1. ♘a6+ ♚a8
2. ♗c6#.

Board 2

> The bishop waits along the h3–c8 diagonal until the king is trapped in the corner. It then delivers checkmate along the h1–a8 diagonal.

Elements

The basic building blocks of chess are referred to as its elements. Each of the elements of the game may be understood individually, but it is their relationships to one another at any point in a game that is difficult to master. Sometimes the relative importance of the elements changes during the course of the game.

Space In many ways chess is a game of spatial conquest. All things being equal, the more room you have to maneuver with, the better off you'll be. Both sides begin a game with the same amount of territory. There is an invisible line of demarcation between the two territories between the 4th and 5th ranks. If you cross it, you may find yourself behind enemy lines!

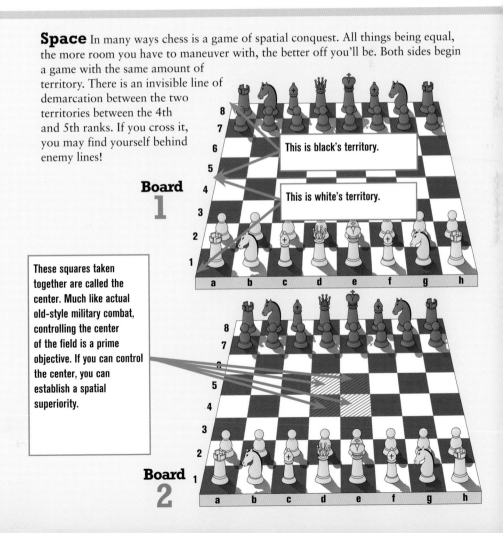

This is black's territory.

This is white's territory.

Board 1

These squares taken together are called the center. Much like actual old-style military combat, controlling the center of the field is a prime objective. If you can control the center, you can establish a spatial superiority.

Board 2

That is one reason why ❶ e4 is the most popular way to open a chess game. It occupies one of the central squares, and attacks another. White is now attacking multiple squares in black's territory with just one move!

Board 3

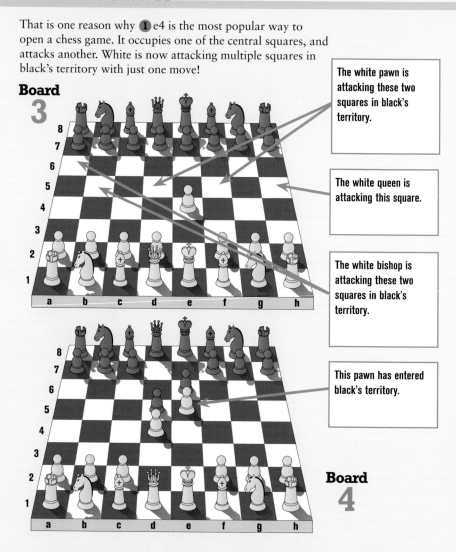

The white pawn is attacking these two squares in black's territory.

The white queen is attacking this square.

The white bishop is attacking these two squares in black's territory.

This pawn has entered black's territory.

Board 4

This position is arrived at following the moves ❶ e4 e6 ❷ d4 d5, and is called the *Advanced Variation of the French Defense*. White has invaded black's territory and seized an advantage in space. The main strategic battle will revolve around white's ability to support this advance and black's attempts to undermine it.

Material Not all chess pieces are created equal. Some are more powerful than others. They draw their strength from their mobility, so it follows that the more mobile the piece the more valuable it is. We use the pawn as the basic unit of force and assign it a value of 1. The other pieces are valued in relation to the pawn, except for the king. The king is of infinite importance, because its loss means the loss of the game.

The Relative Values of the Pieces

PIECE	VALUE
Pawn	1
Knight	3
Bishop	3
Rook	5
Queen	9

Some people suggest valuing the bishop at $3\frac{1}{4}$ in order to give it a slight preference over the knight. The knights can be a bit tricky to master.

Based on this valuation we can see that the queen is worth more than a rook and bishop together, but less than two rooks.

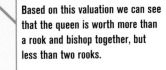

Development There is an element of time in the game of chess, and in the opening stages of the game it is referred to as *development*. The key to development is to move your pieces to their optimal squares as efficiently as possible. Determining which piece belongs where depends largely on what moves your opponent has made. No one said chess was easy!

It's difficult to know where the bishops should be because it often depends on where your opponent's pawns are. You wouldn't move the bishop to f4 if black had a pawn on e5, for example.

Make a minimal number of pawn moves, and choose ones that let you get your pieces off the first rank.

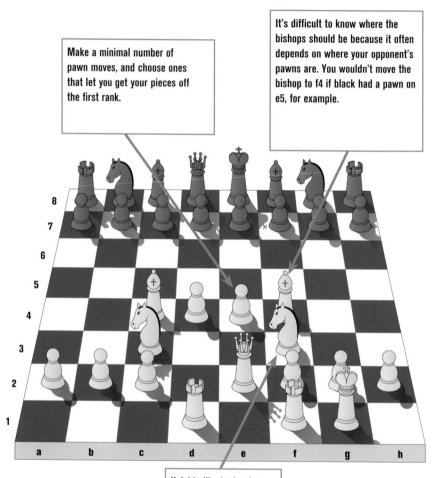

Knights like to develop toward the center and are often initially placed on f3, c3, or both.

Special Moves

When you have mastered the basic movements of the pieces, you are almost ready to play a game. However, there are a few more rules for you to learn before you can play a game properly. Not everyone who believes they know how to play chess knows these rules!

En Passant The en passant rule is probably the last rule most chess players learn, and some never learn it! It is a special move involving only pawns, and stems from the fact that pawns have the option to move either one or two squares on their initial move. If a pawn moves two squares, but passes an enemy pawn on the 5th rank while doing so, the enemy pawn will have the option, but not the obligation, of capturing it. The capture takes place as though the pawn had moved one square only. This option exists for one turn, and is forfeit if not immediately exercised.

This pawn has advanced two squares on its initial move. This gives the pawn on d5 the opportunity to capture it en passant. This is written as e.p. in chess notation.

The white pawn captures as though the black pawn had moved to e6 instead of e5. This capture must be made immediately if it is to be made at all. Any other move by white would forfeit the opportunity to capture en passant.

Board 1

Board 2

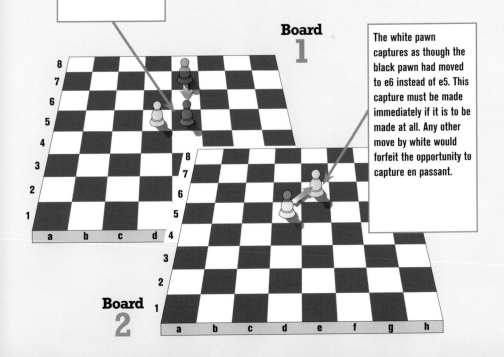

Promotion The pawn has another special attribute called *promotion*. If a pawn reaches the 8th rank, it may be exchanged for any other piece except the king. Since the queen is the most powerful piece, the pawn is usually promoted to a queen. As a pawn approaches the 8th rank, it is said to be approaching its queening square. If you choose to promote to a piece other than the queen, you are said to be underpromoting.

Usually, as a game progresses, more and more pieces get captured. The more pieces get captured the more important the lowly pawn becomes. Its ability to move to the 8th square and promote to other pieces frequently makes the difference near the end of a game.

Castling Castling is the only move in chess where you're allowed to move two pieces at once: the king and rook. There are some restrictions: there must be no other piece between the king and rook; the king cannot be in check, nor pass through or land on a square attacked by an enemy piece; and finally, neither the king nor the rook may have moved prior to castling. If you castle with the a-rook, you are castling on the queenside or "castling long" in chess lingo. This is recorded as 0–0–0 in chess notation. If you castle with the h-rook, you are castling on the kingside or "castling short," recorded as 0–0.

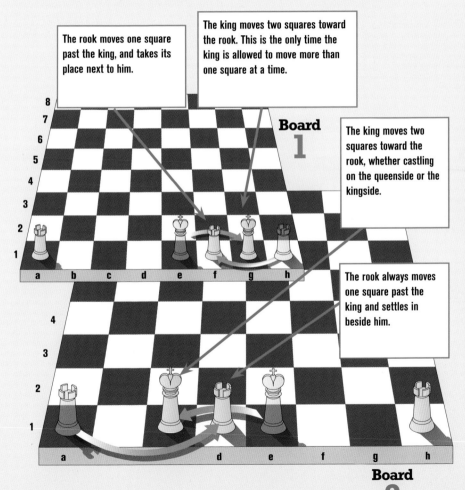

The rook moves one square past the king, and takes its place next to him.

The king moves two squares toward the rook. This is the only time the king is allowed to move more than one square at a time.

The king moves two squares toward the rook, whether castling on the queenside or the kingside.

Board 1

The rook always moves one square past the king and settles in beside him.

Board 2

Mastery Challenges I

☞ For answers, see pp.36 and 37

"Every chess master was once a beginner."

Irving Chernev (1900–1981)

Use this blank chessboard to help you answer questions 1–3.

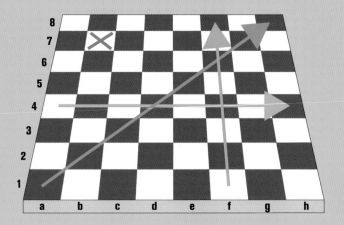

1 **Name the square**
What's the name of the square marked with an X?

2 **Chessboard streets**
Find the lines that identify a file, a rank, and a diagonal.

3 **Set 'em up!**
Imagine the white chess pieces (not pawns) set up on the first rank ready for a game. Using the abbreviations you've learned for the pieces, list them in order from left to right.

4 **Piece values**
Using the list of letter abbreviations you just made, write the relative value of each piece (1–9) underneath each abbreviation. Exception: Score the king with a ∞, because it's infinitely valuable.

5 **Risk and reward**
If a pawn advances through the hazards of battle all the way to the other side of the board, what happens?

6 Check it out

Identify the board that shows a checkmate, a stalemate, and a simple check.

Board A

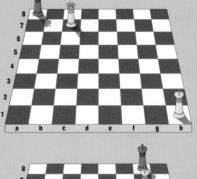

Board B

Board C

7 Castling practice

Set up a chessboard to match the one to the right. Move the pieces to show the position after both sides castle kingside (0–0). Then reset and move the pieces to show the position after both sides castle queenside (0–0–0).

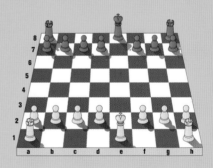

8 A question in passing

In the position shown here, white has just moved e2–e4. Is his pawn in danger?

9 **Look ahead! Knight development**
How many moves does the knight have in Board A
below? How about in Board B?

**Board
A**

**Board
B**

ANSWERS

1 **b7 is the square marked with an X.** To verify this, just follow the
grid of ranks and files marked around the board to their intersection on
the square.

2 **The tan-colored line identifies the f–file. The blue line identifies the
fourth rank. The green line identifies the long dark diagonal.** Always
remember that when you set up the board, you must keep "light on
right!" It's important that h1 and a8 be light squares. Otherwise, the
board position is illegal. Movies, TV, and all kinds of paper and web-
based publishers seem to defy the odds by getting this fact wrong more
than half the time.

3 **R, N, B, Q, K, B, N, R.** Remember that the knight has to be
abbreviated with an N because the king, asserting his royal prerogative,
usurped the K.

4 The values are: **5, 3, 3, 9, ∞, 3, 3, 5.** Keep it simple for now and value knights and bishops the same. But give yourself credit if you assigned the bishops a value of 3¼.

5 **Promotion!** If a pawn makes it alive to the opposite edge of the board, its player can and must replace it with any piece except a king or another pawn. This is normally a glorious moment for the player, and he nearly always chooses to promote to a queen because it is the most powerful piece. And yes, you can have more than one queen!

6 Board B shows a checkmate. A shows a stalemate. C shows a simple check.

7 With both sides castled kingside (0–0), the position becomes that shown in Board A, below. After both sides castle queenside (0–0–0), the position becomes that shown in Board B, below.

Board
A

Board
B

8 **Yes!** If black chooses to capture, he can use the en passant rule. Black would remove the white pawn and move the black pawn to e3. But if he waits even one move, black has lost the opportunity.

9 **In Board A, the knight has eight moves, while in the corner it has only two.** Knights especially have more mobility in the center. And, remember, they're the only pieces that can jump over other chessmen.

Section 2: OPENING PRINCIPLES

Chess play throughout history had been characterized by attacks against enemy kings until the publication of *L'analyze du Jeu des Échecs* by François-André Philidor (1726–1795) in 1749.

Classical Opening Principles

Philidor was ahead of his time, and it wasn't until the latter half of the nineteenth century that players generally accepted the idea that attacks needed to be properly prepared if they were to be successful consistently.

Players learned to postpone immediate attacks against the enemy king in favor of intermediate goals, such as the conquest and control of the center. Direct attacks would only be justified after some strategic advantage had been obtained. The art of defending against premature attacks rose to new heights in the games and writings of Wilhelm Steinitz (1836–1900), who was the first official World Champion.

Centralization The center is the most important part of the chessboard. Pieces placed in the center attack more squares then those positioned on one side or the other. It is often difficult to maneuver pieces from one side of the board to the other if you do not control or possess your fair share of the center.

The four central squares are the most important ones to control.

Board

1

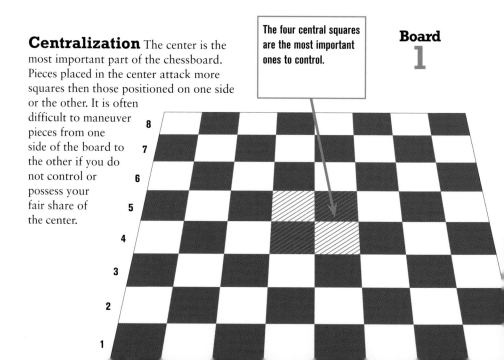

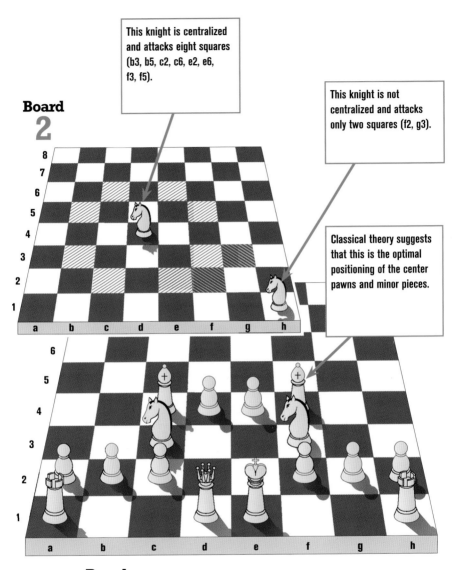

This knight is centralized and attacks eight squares (b3, b5, c2, c6, e2, e6, f3, f5).

This knight is not centralized and attacks only two squares (f2, g3).

Classical theory suggests that this is the optimal positioning of the center pawns and minor pieces.

Board 2

Board 3

Quick Development The principle of quick development was evident in the games of Paul Morphy (1837–1884), and codified in the writings of Siegbert Tarrasch (1862–1934). Tarrasch emphasized the dynamic mobility of the pieces over the relatively static positioning of pawns.

It was considered important to get the minor pieces (knights and bishops) out before developing the major pieces (rooks and queen). Ideally, you would make the minimum number of pawn moves that allowed you to develop all of your pieces from their original squares.

Notice that both of white's bishops are free to move, but this bishop is not.

This pawn has moved twice already: e7–e5, e5×d4.

Board

1

Black has violated a classical opening principle by developing the queen before the minor pieces.

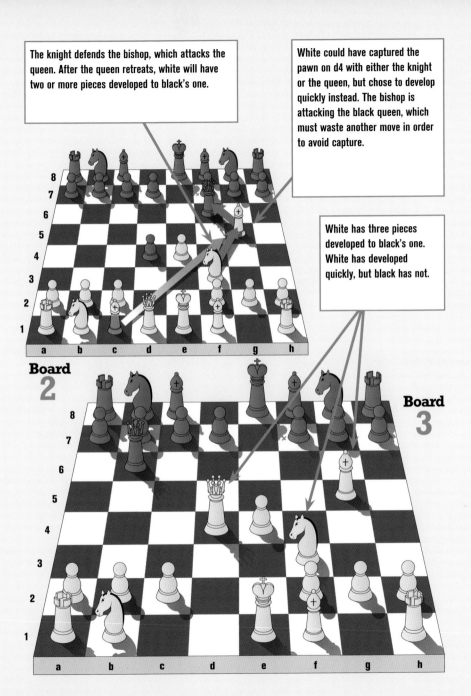

The knight defends the bishop, which attacks the queen. After the queen retreats, white will have two or more pieces developed to black's one.

White could have captured the pawn on d4 with either the knight or the queen, but chose to develop quickly instead. The bishop is attacking the black queen, which must waste another move in order to avoid capture.

White has three pieces developed to black's one. White has developed quickly, but black has not.

Board
2

Board
3

Castle Early Another classical principle related to centralization was the suggestion to castle early. If the center of the board was to be the main theater of combat, it stood to reason that the king should be sheltered somewhere else.

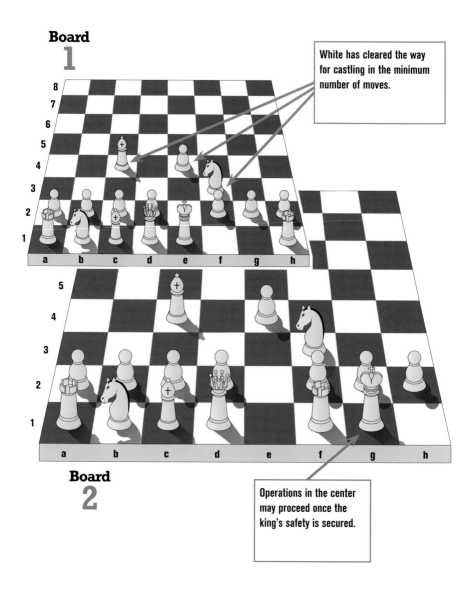

Board 1

White has cleared the way for castling in the minimum number of moves.

Board 2

Operations in the center may proceed once the king's safety is secured.

Knights Before Bishops Another classical opening principle
was to develop your knights before your bishops. It's difficult to know the
optimal placement for pieces, such as the bishop, until you see which
pawns are moved where. With the knights, on the other hand, you
generally know where they should be. One of former World Champion
José Capablanca's (1888–1942) maxims was to develop at least one
knight before bringing out the bishops.

This knight's natural square
is f3, where it can bring to
bear the most influence on
the center.

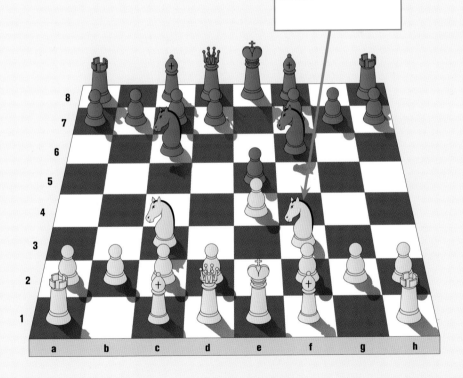

Modern Opening Principles

The classic understanding of opening principles came under attack in the 1920s by what became known as the "Hypermodern School." One of the core contributions to chess theory was the principle of control rather than occupation of the center.

The center of the chess world moved to the former Soviet Union in the 1940s where the synthesis of the classical and hypermodern schools of thought became known as the Soviet School of Chess.

In reality the shift was not to a new school of thought, but to a reliance on concrete analysis in order to determine a move's utility. Moves which produced weaknesses according to the old theories were played with abandon if it could be demonstrated through analysis that the weaknesses could not be exploited. Nowadays, anything goes as long as it works!

Control Versus Occupation

Example 1: The King's Indian Defense (☛ see also p.82) must have come as a shock to classical players when it first appeared in tournament play. The moves ① d4 ♘f6 ② c4 g6 ③ ♘c3 ♗g7 ④ e4 d6 seem to concede the center to white. However, black allows white to occupy the center with pawns with the idea of attacking and weakening them later.

This bishop indirectly attacks the center squares e5 and d4. It sits on a safe perch and attacks from long range.

Board

1

Pawns under attack may advance. This often secures a spatial advantage, which would be enough to convince a classical player of the superiority of white's position. However, modern theory considers an additional fact: pawns which become fixed in position can be easy targets to attack.

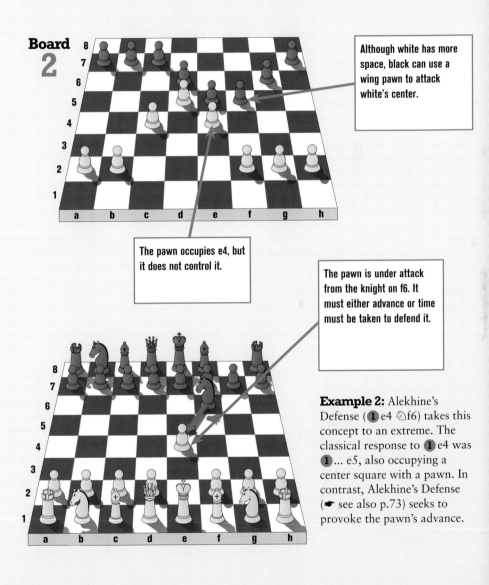

Board 2

Although white has more space, black can use a wing pawn to attack white's center.

The pawn occupies e4, but it does not control it.

The pawn is under attack from the knight on f6. It must either advance or time must be taken to defend it.

Example 2: Alekhine's Defense (**1** e4 ♞f6) takes this concept to an extreme. The classical response to **1** e4 was **1** ... e5, also occupying a center square with a pawn. In contrast, Alekhine's Defense (☞ see also p.73) seeks to provoke the pawn's advance.

The Initiative If you can consistently force your opponent to react in specific ways to your moves, you are said to have the *initiative*. The initiative can be lost with a single passive move.

Example 1: After the moves **1** e4 e5 **2** ♘f3 white is trying to force black to defend the pawn on e5.

Board 1

If black defends the pawn by playing **2**... ♘c6, white can continue to try to force black's hand with **3** ♗b5 (this is called the *Ruy Lopez*, ☞ see also p.57). White attacks the pawn's defender and tries to keep dictating black's play. White is using the initiative that results from having the first move. This is a very slight advantage, but in the hands of Grandmasters it is a little like having the serve in tennis.

Board 2

This knight defends the pawn on e5 from the attack by the knight on f3.

This bishop attacks the knight, which defends the pawn.

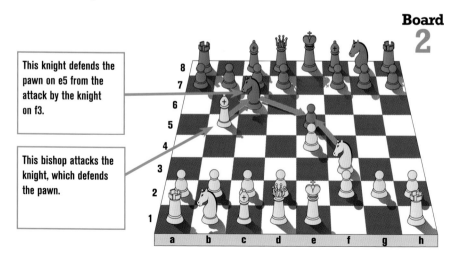

Example 2: Black has other ways to respond to white's threat. Petroff's Defense (☛ see also p.64), ➊ e4 e5 ➋ ♘f3 ♘f6, seeks to counter white's threat with one of black's own.

Black threatens white's pawn on e4 instead of defending the one on e5.

Board 1

If white captures the pawn with ➌ ♘xe5, black responds by playing ➌... d6, forcing white to move the knight. Now it is black who is dictating white's play. Once white's knight retreats, black can take the pawn on e4, restoring material balance. (Note: the copycat strategy ➋... ♘xe4 is bad, because after ➌ ♕e2 ♕e7 4 ♕xe4 black cannot play ➍... ♕xe5. Copycat strategies are nearly always bad.)

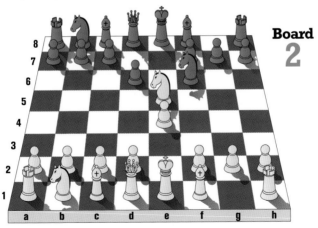

Board 2

Both the Ruy Lopez and Petroff's Defense are solid choices against white's threat. They illustrate two differing means of reacting to white's early initiative: defense and counterattack.

Counterplay Equilibrium exists on the chessboard before the game begins, but it is disturbed when white makes the first move. This move gives white the early initiative. Black may seek to reestablish equilibrium with each response (meeting **1** e4 with **1** ... e5 for example), but modern theory suggests that it becomes more difficult to continue to do this as the game progresses.

An alternative would be to inject imbalances into the position, so that it becomes more difficult for white to profit from the right to move first. White should still hold a theoretical edge, however black responds, but imbalances produce greater practical chances for the second player.

Example 1: The Sicilian Defense **1** e4 c5 (☛ see also p.68) establishes an imbalance immediately.

Board 1

This queen is free to move to the queenside.

This queen is free to move to the kingside.

This bishop is free to move, while its counterpart on c8 is not.

After a standard continuation (**2** ♘f3 ♞c6 **3** d4 c×d4 **4** ♘×d4), we can see that white's pieces have more open lines at their disposal. It will be easier to develop them quickly. Black, on the other hand, has two center pawns to white's one. This means that black's long-term prospects for controlling the center are enhanced. White must try to capitalize on this short-term advantage in development before black can catch up.

Black has a central advantage of two pawns to one.

Board 2

If we clear away all the pieces (but not the pawns) from the position, another imbalance becomes clear. White has a clear path into black's territory along the d-file. Black has the c-file to use to attack white's position. Each side's rooks will naturally gravitate to these half-open files.

Board 3

This bishop is important to black's defense of the kingside, and white wants to eliminate it.

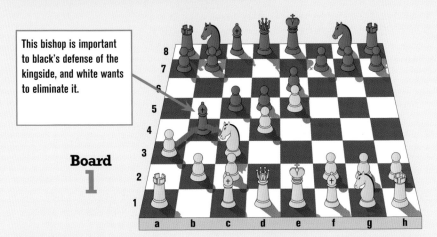

Board 1

Example 2: This is a position from the Winawer Variation of the French Defense (☞ see also p.71). The moves were **1** e4 e6 **2** d4 d5 **3** ♘c3 ♝b4 **4** e5 c5 **5** a3. White has just attacked the black bishop in order to force it to retreat or exchange itself for the knight on c3.

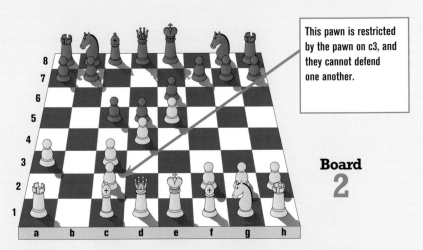

This pawn is restricted by the pawn on c3, and they cannot defend one another.

Board 2

Black is willing to trade the bishop for the knight (**5** ... ♝xc3+ **6** bxc3), because in turn white's queenside pawn structure is disrupted. White will have the advantage on the kingside, while black will hold an edge on the queenside.

Positional Sacrifices

There were plenty of sacrifices in games conducted under classical principles. These sacrifices were made in the spirit of attack. Modern opening principles allow for a second type of sacrifice: a positional sacrifice. The intent is not to launch an early violent attack, but to gain some strategic advantage, which can only be exploited over time. One such example is the Benko Gambit.

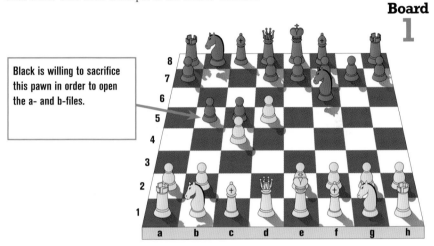

Board 1

Black is willing to sacrifice this pawn in order to open the a- and b-files.

This diagram shows the defining moves of the Benko Gambit:
1 d4 ♘f6 **2** c4 c5 **3** d5 b5.

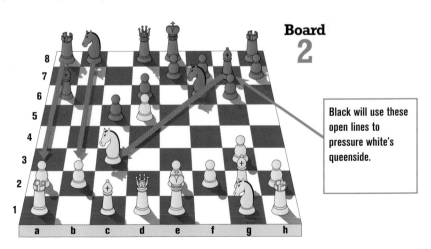

Board 2

Black will use these open lines to pressure white's queenside.

A typical continuation might be:
4 c×b5 a6 **5** b×a6 g6 **6** ♘c3 ♗×a6 **7** g3 d6 **8** ♗g2 ♗g7.

Mastery Challenges II

☞ For answers, see p.55

"Help your pieces so they can help you."

Paul Morphy (1837–1884)

1 **Prime real estate**
In the opening of a chess game, which four squares make up the most important territory?

2 **Development**
Using what you've learned about classical ideas, in the position below, suggest the best piece move for white.

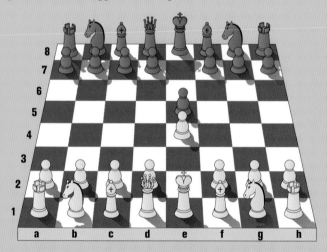

3 **Opening tips**
From this list of six, choose the three most important things to keep in mind when beginning a chess game:

A. Make one or two central pawn moves.

B. Keep your pieces on the kingside.

C. Intimidate your opponent by making early attacking moves.

D. Develop your knights and bishops to squares that bear on the center.

E. Push your a– and h–pawns as a flank attack.

F. Castle early.

4 Occupation versus control

Which position shows the classical chess idea of central *occupation*? Which shows the modern idea of central *control*?

Board A

Board B

5 Investing in the initiative

In the position below, how can white gambit a pawn in return for an opening initiative?

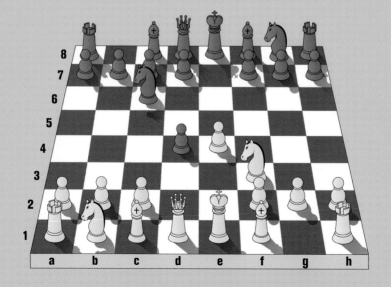

6 Modern counterplay

Many modern masters playing black create counterplay by choosing imbalanced openings. Which position is an example of that approach?

Board A

Board B

7 Look ahead! Closed/open games

One of the opening positions below reveals lots of paths available for both sides' pieces. This kind of position is called an "open" game. The other has a more congested quality, calling for maneuvering rather than direct contact. This kind of position is called a "closed" game. You'll study these ideas in the next section. But use what you've already learned to identify which is which.

Board A

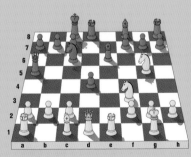

Board B

ANSWERS

1 The most important squares on the chessboard are e4, d4, e5, and d5—the four squares in the very center. The board's center is the equivalent of the military "high ground." In more peaceful terms, it's "prime real estate." In the center, chess pieces have more mobility and control more squares. If you control the center, it's easier for you to shift your army quickly.

2 Nf3 is the best developing move available on the board:
- It attacks the black pawn on e5 and therefore develops an initiative by forcing black to go on the defensive.
- It puts the knight in a position to strike at the central squares.
- It follows the principle "knight before bishop."

3 A, D, and F. Know these three rules for the opening by heart and you'll avoid early catastrophes.
- Make only one or two pawn moves that occupy or control the center.
- Develop your pieces—that means get them off the back rank and onto squares that hit the center.
- Castle! It brings your vulnerable king into safety and your powerful rook toward the center.

4 Board B shows the classical occupation of the central square. A exemplifies the modern idea of central control.

5 White could gambit a pawn with 4. c3 (rather than recapture the pawn with 4. Nxd4). If black then plays 4. ... dxc3, white could respond 5. Nxc3. He would be a pawn down—but ahead in development.

6 Board A illustrates the modern idea of anticipating counterplay by creating imbalanced positions out of the opening.

7 Board B is the open game. Notice the diagonals with many squares available for the bishops, and the files that will be available for the rooks. A is the closed game—both sides here will need to maneuver to find pathways to the enemy.

Section 3: GAME TYPES

Chess openings are divided into types which share similar characteristics. There is usually more room for piece movement in open types than in closed types.

Open Games

According to convention, games that begin ① e4 e5 are called open games.

Ruy Lopez Also called the *Spanish Game*, the Ruy Lopez is one of the oldest of all chess openings.

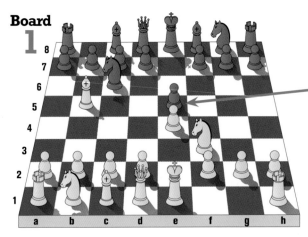

Board 1

Black seeks to maintain control over the e5 square in order to ensure a fair share of the center.

The moves that define the Ruy Lopez are: ① e4 e5 ② ♘f3 ♘c6 ③ ♗b5.

Board 2

In the Closed Variation of the Ruy Lopez, black forces white to take time to defend the pawn on e4. The game is usually characterized by subtle maneuverings rather than violent attacks.

The following moves are typical of the Closed Variation: ③ ... a6 ④ ♗a4 ♘f6 ⑤ 0–0 ♗e7 ⑥ ♖e1 b5 ⑦ ♗b3 d6 ⑧ c3 0–0.

Ruy Lopez: Open Variation

Board 1

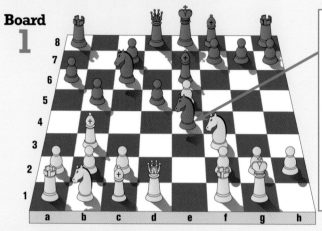

In the Open Variation of the Ruy Lopez, black captures the pawn on e4, even if it means losing the pawn on e5. The disappearance of these pawns opens the game up for the pieces to quickly come to blows.

This is the Open Variation of the Ruy Lopez:
1 e4 e5 **2** ♘f3 ♘c6 **3** ♗b5 a6
4 ♗a4 ♘f6 **5** 0–0 ♘xe4.

Black has a four-to-three pawn advantage on the queenside. If black can mobilize this pawn majority in time, it will distract white from the planned kingside attack.

This advanced pawn gives white a spatial advantage on the kingside, which improves white's attacking chances.

Board 2

A typical continuation would be: **6** d4 b5 **7** ♗b3 d5 **8** dxe5 ♗e6.

Ruy Lopez: Berlin Defense

The Berlin Defense is considered somewhat old-fashioned, but it is sound nevertheless.

Board 1

> In the Berlin Defense, black plays **3** ... ♞f6 in order to threaten white's pawn on e4.

The Berlin Defense begins:
1 e4 e5
2 ♞f3 ♞c6
3 ♝b5 ♞f6.

> Black's king has been forced to move, and will be less secure than white's.

> White has a healthy pawn majority on the kingside, while black's queenside majority is crippled.

Board 2

> Black will have two bishops versus bishop and knight. The two bishops are more effective in open positions, such as this one.

This is the usual continuation:
4 0–0 ♞xe4 **5** d4 ♞d6 **6** ♝xc6 dxc6 **7** dxe5 ♞f5 **8** ♛xd8+ ♚xd8.

Giuoco Piano

Giuoco Piano Also known as the *Italian Game*, the Giuoco Piano is quite logical. However, experience has shown that it packs less of a punch than the Ruy Lopez.

The bishops are developed to active squares, but they are also more exposed than they might otherwise be.

The opening moves are:
1 e4 e5 **2** ♘f3 ♘c6 **3** ♗c4 ♗c5.

Board 1

Board 2

White has sacrificed a pawn, but has obtained good attacking chances as a result. Notice how white has four pieces developed and has castled. Black only has two pieces developed and has not yet castled. Aggressive players prefer to have white in this position, while materialists prefer black.

Here is a possible continuation:
4 c3 ♘f6 **5** d4 exd4 **6** cxd4 ♗b4+ **7** ♘c3 ♘xe4
8 0–0 ♗xc3 **9** d5 ♗f6 **10** ♖e1 ♘e7 **11** ♖xe4 d6 **12** ♗g5.

Evans Gambit This opening was a favorite of Paul Morphy, who was one of the greatest players of all time. It sacrifices material for a lead in development and a central pawn advantage. The opening became less popular as defensive techniques began to improve.

Board 1

The pawn is undefended, but black must lose some time in capturing it. The pawn also deflects the bishop away from the center.

These moves define the Evans Gambit:
1 e4 e5 **2** ♘f3 ♘c6 **3** ♗c4 ♗c5 **4** b4.

Board 2

In return for the sacrificed pawn, white has secured a strong pawn center and established a lead in development. Notice that white has already castled, but that black has not. However, if black ever catches up in development, the sacrificed pawn may come back to haunt white.

One possible continuation is:
4 ... ♗xb4 **5** c3 ♗a5 **6** d4 d6 **7** 0-0 exd4 **8** cxd4 ♗b6.

Two Knights Defense

Black is not obligated to meet white's ③ ♗c4 with ③... ♗c5. The alternative ③... ♘f6 leads to the Two Knights Defense.

Board 1

If you choose to play the Two Knights Defense, you must be ready to handle white's aggressive fourth move. The knight on g5 and the bishop on c4 both attack the black pawn on f7. There is no adequate way to defend it directly.

One variation of the Two Knights Defense starts with:
① e4 e5 ② ♘f3 ♘c6 ③ ♗c4 ♘f6 ④ ♘g5.

In this case it is black who has the lead in development and nice open lines for the pieces. White, on the other hand, has the extra pawn.

Board 2

A popular continuation is:
④... d5 ⑤ exd5 ♘a5 ⑥ ♗b5+ c6
⑦ dxc6 bxc6 ⑧ ♗e2 h6 ⑨ ♘f3 ♗d6.

Two Knights Defense continued

Board 3

White may also play the safer ④ d4, challenging black's share of the center.

An alternative to ④ ♘g5 is: ④ d4.

Board 4

Again we see the contrasting advantages of white's kingside pawn majority versus black's two bishops.

The following is a typical continuation:
④... exd4 ⑤ e5 d5 ⑥ ♗b5 ♘e4 ⑦ ♘xd4 ♗d7 ⑧ ♗xc6 bxc6.

Scotch Game

Chess openings go in and out of style, just as things do in the world of fashion. The Scotch was once quite popular and then fell out of favor. In the 1990s it became all the rage again when World Champion Gary Kasparov scored some impressive wins with it, but it has since lost some of its luster. It is only a matter of time before it comes back into style.

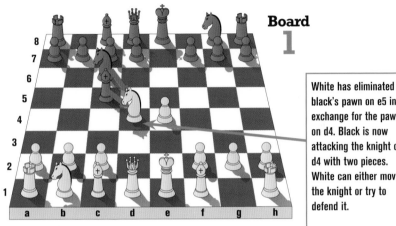

Board 1

White has eliminated black's pawn on e5 in exchange for the pawn on d4. Black is now attacking the knight on d4 with two pieces. White can either move the knight or try to defend it.

Variation 1: One variation of the Scotch Game is:
1 e4 e5 **2** ♘f3 ♘c6 **3** d4 exd4 **4** ♘xd4 ♗c5.

Black will be able to complete development comfortably, but white's pawn on e4 will provide a small, yet lasting, spatial advantage.

Board 2

Here is a typical continuation:
5 ♗e3 ♛f6 **6** c3 ♘ge7 **7** ♗c4 0–0 **8** 0–0 ♗b6.

Petroff's Defense Black is not obligated to defend the pawn on e5 when white attacks it. An alternative is to counterattack the white pawn on e4. That is the idea behind Petroff's Defense, which is also known as the *Russian Game*.

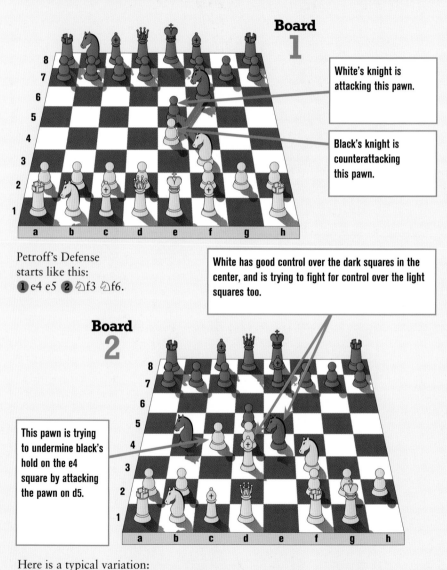

Board 1

White's knight is attacking this pawn.

Black's knight is counterattacking this pawn.

Petroff's Defense starts like this:
1 e4 e5 **2** ♘f3 ♘f6.

White has good control over the dark squares in the center, and is trying to fight for control over the light squares too.

Board 2

This pawn is trying to undermine black's hold on the e4 square by attacking the pawn on d5.

Here is a typical variation:
3 ♘xe5 d6 **4** ♘f3 ♘xe4 **5** d4 d5 **6** ♗d3 ♗e7 **7** 0–0 ♘c6 **8** c4 ♘b4.

King's Gambit This is another very old opening, which has fallen out of favor. The King's Gambit was a favorite choice of attack-minded players until defenses became more sophisticated. The modern view is that the King's Gambit is a bit rash, because it weakens the white king as early as the second move.

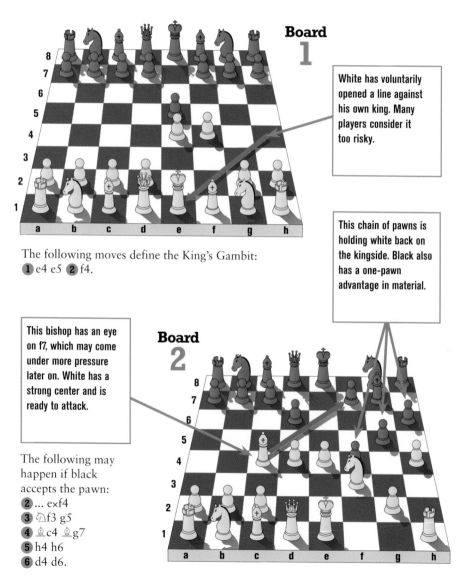

Board 1

White has voluntarily opened a line against his own king. Many players consider it too risky.

The following moves define the King's Gambit:
1 e4 e5 **2** f4.

This chain of pawns is holding white back on the kingside. Black also has a one-pawn advantage in material.

This bishop has an eye on f7, which may come under more pressure later on. White has a strong center and is ready to attack.

Board 2

The following may happen if black accepts the pawn:
2 ... exf4
3 ♘f3 g5
4 ♗c4 ♗g7
5 h4 h6
6 d4 d6.

Vienna Game The queen's knight develops first in the Vienna Game, which may seem less aggressive at first glance. However, the option to play f2–f4 at some point may lead to tactical fireworks later on.

White's strategy is to secure the light squares in the center first and contest the dark ones later.

Board

1

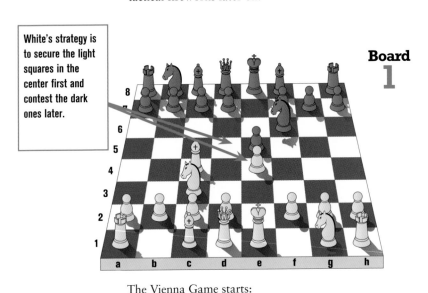

The Vienna Game starts:
1 e4 e5 **2** ♘c3 ♘f6 **3** ♗c4.

Black owns the bishop pair.

These pawns help white to control the center.

Board

2

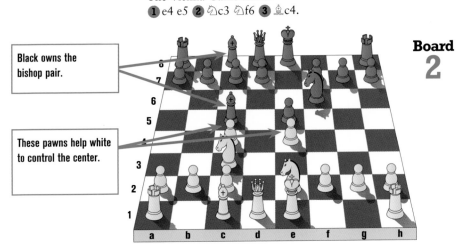

This is one possible continuation:
3... ♘c6 **4** d3 ♘a5 **5** ♘ge2 ♘xc4 **6** dxc4 ♗c5.

Danish Gambit

White's objective in the Danish Gambit is an early violent attack.

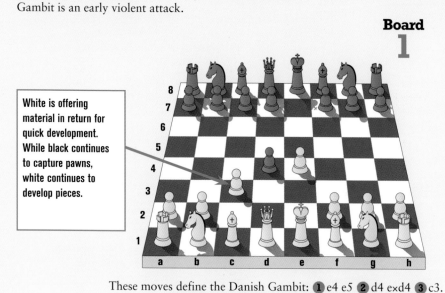

White is offering material in return for quick development. While black continues to capture pawns, white continues to develop pieces.

These moves define the Danish Gambit: **1** e4 e5 **2** d4 exd4 **3** c3.

Black has three queenside pawns.

White has only one queenside pawn.

A possible continuation might be:
3 ... dxc3 **4** ♗c4 cxb2 **5** ♗xb2 d5 **6** ♗xd5 ♘f6 **7** ♗xf7+ ♚xf7
8 ♛xd8 ♗b4+ **9** ♛d2 ♗xd2+ **10** ♘xd2 c5.

After the smoke clears, we can see that although material equality has been reestablished an imbalance remains. White has a four-to-two majority of pawns on the kingside, while black has a three-to-one advantage on the queenside.

Semi-Open Games

The term *semi-open* applies to openings where white's ① e4 is met by some other move than ① ... e5. These openings tend to be less symmetrical than the open games. Imbalances are more likely to arise early and a wide variety of strategies may be used.

This is the Najdorf Variation of the Sicilian Defense.

Sicilian Defense The Sicilian Defense is the most popular of all chess openings. It establishes asymmetry at once with ① e4 c5.

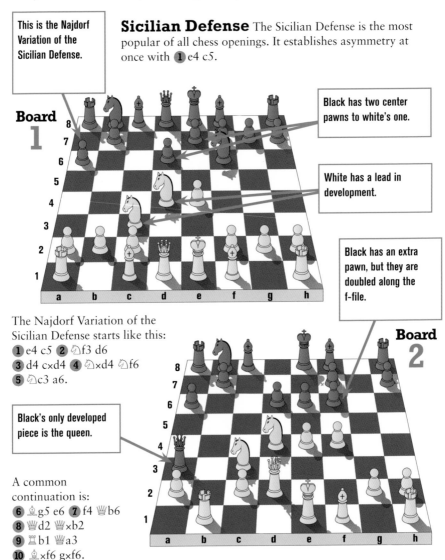

Board 1

Black has two center pawns to white's one.

White has a lead in development.

Black has an extra pawn, but they are doubled along the f-file.

The Najdorf Variation of the Sicilian Defense starts like this:
① e4 c5 ② ♘f3 d6
③ d4 cxd4 ④ ♘xd4 ♘f6
⑤ ♘c3 a6.

Black's only developed piece is the queen.

Board 2

A common continuation is:
⑥ ♗g5 e6 ⑦ f4 ♕b6
⑧ ♕d2 ♕xb2
⑨ ♖b1 ♕a3
⑩ ♗xf6 gxf6.

Sicilian Defense: Dragon Variation

If black plays
5 ... g6 instead of
5 ... a6 it is called
the Dragon Variation.

Board 1

The Dragon Variation starts like this:
1 e4 c5 **2** ♘f3 d6 **3** d4 cxd4 **4** ♘xd4 ♘f6 **5** ♘c3 g6.

Since black's c-pawn has been removed, the rook will have an open line into white's territory.

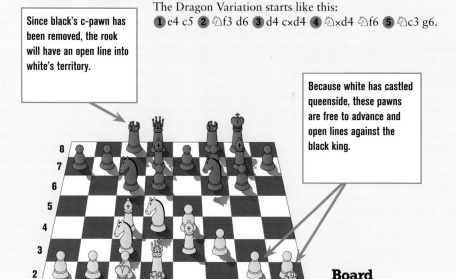

Because white has castled queenside, these pawns are free to advance and open lines against the black king.

Board 2

A typical variation might be:
6 ♗e3 ♗g7 **7** f3 ♘c6 **8** ♕d2 0–0 **9** ♗c4 ♗d7 **10** 0–0–0 ♖c8.

Sicilian Defense: Alapin Variation

Board 1

With this move, white is preparing to play d2–d4. If black captures on d4, white intends to recapture with a pawn instead of a piece.

The Alapin Variation is defined by the following moves:
1 e4 c5 **2** c3.

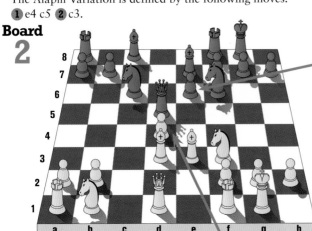

Board 2

Black has less of a foothold in the center than white, because this pawn is not attacking any squares in white's territory.

This pawn is isolated. It must be defended by white's pieces or be lost.

This is a typical variation:
2 ... d5
3 e×d5 ♕×d5
4 d4 ♘f6
5 ♘f3 e6
6 ♗d3 ♗e7
7 0–0 0×0
8 ♗e3 c×d4
9 c×d4 ♘c6.

French Defense

French Defense The French Defense to white's **1** e4 is **1**... e6. Black intends to play **2**... d5 and fight for control over the light squares in the center.

French Defense: Winawer Variation

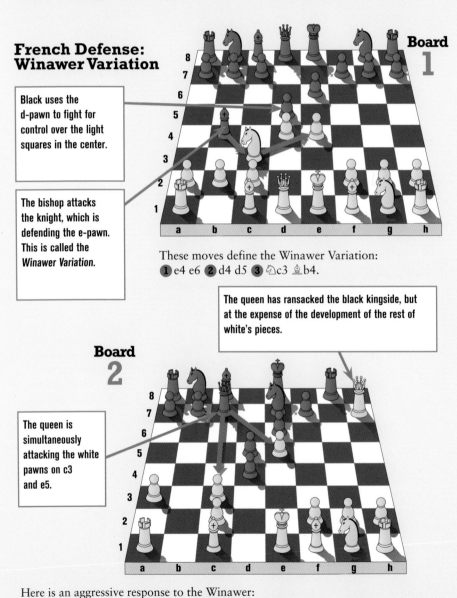

Black uses the d-pawn to fight for control over the light squares in the center.

The bishop attacks the knight, which is defending the e-pawn. This is called the *Winawer Variation.*

These moves define the Winawer Variation:
1 e4 e6 **2** d4 d5 **3** ♘c3 ♗b4.

The queen has ransacked the black kingside, but at the expense of the development of the rest of white's pieces.

Board 2

The queen is simultaneously attacking the white pawns on c3 and e5.

Here is an aggressive response to the Winawer:
4 e5 c5 **5** a3 ♗xc3+ **6** bxc3 ♕c7 **7** ♕g4 ♘e7 **8** ♕xg7 ♖g8 **9** ♕xh7 cxd4.

Caro–Kann Defense
The Caro–Kann Defense counters white's **1** e4 with **1** … c6. Black will play a later d7–d5 in order to challenge white's control of the center.

Black is contesting white's control over these central squares.

Board 1

This is a popular way to play the Caro–Kann:
1 e4 c6 **2** d4 d5 **3** ♘c3 dxe4 **4** ♘xe4 ♘f6.

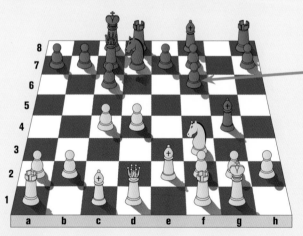

This pawn is doubled, but it does help guard the e5 square, and the g-file is open for use against white's king.

Board 2

This is how play might develop:
5 ♘xf6 gxf6 **6** ♘f3 ♗g4 **7** ♗e2 ♕c7 **8** 0-0 ♘d7 **9** c4 0-0-0.

Alekhine's Defense Alekhine's Defense is one of the more provocative chess openings. Black dares white to advance the center pawns, and even loses time as they advance. Black's idea is that these pawns will become targets that can be undermined later.

There is nothing to prevent white from advancing this pawn and attacking the knight on f6.

Board 1

Black plays Alekhine's Defense: **1** e4 ♞f6.

Board 2

Black has allowed white to occupy the center with pawns in the hope that they will become a defensive liability. Black will pressurize the pawns with active piece play.

A standard variation of Alekhine's Defense:
2 e5 ♞d5 **3** d4 d6 **4** c4 ♞b6 **5** f4 dxe5 **6** fxe5 ♞c6.

Pirc Defense

The Pirc Defense also seems to give white a free hand in the center, however, it has still proven to be a reliable defense. Black postpones an immediate clash in the center, with the hope of initiating one at a more favorable time.

The pawn on d6 helps restrain the advance of white's e-pawn.

Board 1

The Pirc Defense starts like this: **1** e4 d6 **2** d4 ♘f6.

The basic struggle in many modern openings is over the attack and defense of a pawn center. White's d-pawn cannot advance because the e-pawn would be lost. If white's center holds, black's game will be cramped. However, if white's center falls, black's pieces will be more actively placed.

Board 2

A possible continuation:
3 ♘c3 g6 **4** f4 ♗g7 **5** ♘f3 0–0 **6** ♗d3 ♘c6
7 e5 dxe5 **8** fxe5 ♘h5 **9** ♗e3 ♗g4.

Closed Games

Games that begin **1** d4 are generally characterized as closed. This does not mean that the positions cannot be opened, just that they remain closed more often. Closed games place an emphasis on subtle maneuvering rather than on flashy tactics.

Queen's Gambit This is one of the most popular openings, and one frequently seen at the very highest levels of play.

White intends to bring pressure on d5 in the hope of securing the lion's share of the center.

If black captures this pawn, it is called the *Queen's Gambit Accepted*. If black does not capture, or delays capturing the pawn, it is called the *Queen's Gambit Declined*.

Board 1

White plays the Queen's Gambit: **1** d4 d5 **2** c4.

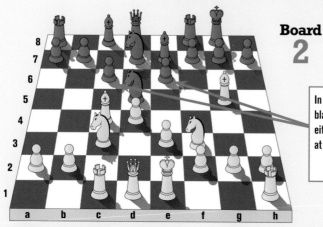

Board 2

In order to equalize, black will have to play either c6-c5 or e6-e5 at some point.

This is a typical variation:
2 ... e6 **3** ♘c3 ♘f6 **4** ♗g5 ♗e7 **5** e3 0–0 **6** ♘f3 ♘bd7 **7** ♖c1 c6 **8** ♗d3 dxc4 **9** ♗xc4 ♘d5.

Queen's Gambit Declined: Exchange Variation

This opening is characterized by an early exchange of pawns on d5.

Board 1

The c-file is half open for white's pieces, while black can use the e-file.

White will push the queenside pawns in order to create weaknesses in black's position. This is called a minority attack, because black actually has more pawns on the queenside than white does.

The Exchange Variation begins like this:
1 d4 d5 **2** c4 e6 **3** ♘c3 ♘f6 **4** cxd5 exd5.

Board 2

A typical variation might be: **5** ♗g5 c6
6 ♕c2 ♗e7 **7** e3 ♘bd7
8 ♗d3 0–0 **9** ♘f3 ♖e8
10 0–0 ♘f8 **11** ♖ab1 g6.

Queen's Gambit Accepted

Board 1

Black accepts the Queen's Gambit by capturing white's c-pawn.

Black accepts the Queen's Gambit: **1** d4 d5 **2** c4 d×c4 **3** ♘f3 ♘f6.

This square will be a good outpost for white's pieces.

Black will probably try to place a knight on this square in order to block the advance of white's d-pawn.

A typical variation:
4 e3 e6 **5** ♗×c4 c5 **6** 0–0 ♘c6
7 ♕e2 c×d4 **8** ♖d1 ♗e7 **9** e×d4.

Board 2

Slav Defense

The Slav is similar to the Queen's Gambit Declined but the c8-bishop is able to move along the h3–c8 diagonal.

Board
1

If black chooses to defend the pawn on d5 with the c-pawn, the opening is called the *Slav Defense*.

The Slav Defense is defined by the moves:
1 d4 d5 **2** c4 c6.

This bishop gets developed before black plays e7-e6. It helps to control the key central square e4.

White has two center pawns to black's one.

Board
2

Play might continue:
3 ♘f3 ♘f6
4 ♘c3 dxc4
5 a4 ♗f5
6 e3 e6
7 ♗xc4 ♗b4.

Queen's Indian Defense

Black fianchetto's the queen bishop in this defense, with an eye toward controlling the center from a distance.

This early pawn move characterizes the Queen's Indian Defense. Black will position the c8 bishop along the h1–a8 diagonal, keeping an eye on the light squares in the center: d5 and e4.

The Queen's Indian Defense begins:
1 d4 ♘f6 **2** c4 e6 **3** ♘f3 b6.

The strategic battle in the Queen's Indian Defense is for control of the e4 square.

Board

2

Play might continue like this:
4 g3 ♗b7 **5** ♗g2 ♗e7 **6** 0–0 0–0 **7** ♘c3 ♘e4.

Nimzo-Indian Defense
Aaron Nimzowitsch popularized this opening, which still bears his name.

Board 1

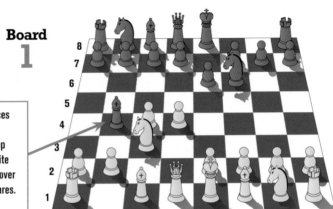

This move introduces the Nimzo-Indian Defense. The bishop neutralizes the white knight's influence over the e4 and d5 squares.

Example 1: The Nimzo-Indian is defined by:
1 d4 ♘f6 **2** c4 e6
3 ♘c3 ♗b4.

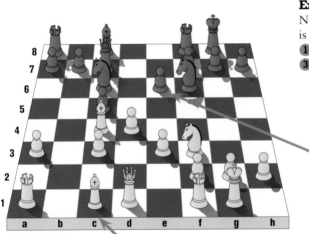

Black can challenge in the center by playing e6–e5, which also activates the bishop on c8.

This bishop is blocked by all the white pawns on dark squares. If white can activate it, the two bishops will work well together.

Board 2

One possible continuation is:
4 e3 c5 **5** ♗d3 0–0 **6** ♘f3 d5
7 0–0 ♘c6 **8** a3 ♗xc3
9 bxc3 dxc4 **10** ♗xc4 ♕c7.

Nimzo-Indian Defense continued

Board 1

The queen can recapture on c3 if black takes the knight, which will preserve white's pawn structure. This is sometimes called the *Capablanca Variation*, after former World Champion José Capablanca.

Example 2: Another way to play the Nimzo-Indian is:
1 d4 ♘f6 **2** c4 e6 **3** ♘c3 ♗b4 **4** ♕c2.

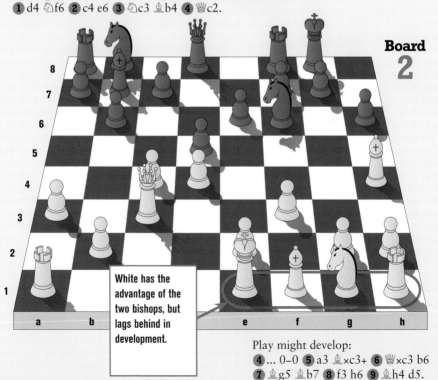

Board 2

White has the advantage of the two bishops, but lags behind in development.

Play might develop:
4 ... 0–0 **5** a3 ♗xc3+ **6** ♕xc3 b6
7 ♗g5 ♗b7 **8** f3 h6 **9** ♗h4 d5.

King's Indian Defense In the King's Indian Defense black seeks to quickly develop the kingside pieces and castle short. Once castled, black will strike out at whatever setup white has chosen.

Board

1

Black's d-pawn restrains the advance of white's e-pawn. Black is ready to castle and then strike back at the white center with either e7–e5 or c7–c5.

The King's Indian Defense starts like this:
1 d4 ♞f6 **2** c4 g6 **3** ♞c3 ♝g7 **4** e4 d6.

Board

2

In the Classical Variation of the King's Indian Defense the center becomes locked. White will attack on the queenside and black on the kingside.

A typical continuation of the Classical Variation:
5 ♞f3 0–0 **6** ♝e2 e5
7 0–0 ♞c6 **8** d5 ♞e7.

King's Indian Defense: Sämisch Variation

Board 1

In this variation of the King's Indian, white uses the f-pawn to guard the e-pawn.

The Sämisch Variation starts:
1 d4 ♞f6 **2** c4 g6 **3** ♞c3 ♝g7 **4** e4 d6 **5** f3.

Board 2

Black must challenge white in the center and on the kingside.

Play might continue:
5 ... 0–0 **6** ♝e3 e5 **7** d5 c6 **8** ♝d3 cxd5 **9** cxd5 ♞e8 **10** ♛d2 f5.

Grünfeld Defense The Grünfeld strategy is also based on first allowing white to establish a pawn center and then attacking it.

Board 1

This pawn is often exchanged for the white pawn on c4. White usually establishes a strong central pawn formation, which black attacks.

Example 1: The Grünfeld Defense begins:
1 d4 ♞f6 **2** c4 g6 **3** ♞c3 d5.

Board 2

There is considerable tension in the center in this position. It occurs in what is referred to as the *Exchange Variation*. The struggle revolves around the attack and defense of white's pawn center.

A common continuation is:
4 cxd5 ♞xd5 **5** e4 ♞xc3 **6** bxc3 ♝g7
7 ♝c4 0–0 **8** ♞e2 c5.

Benoni Defense

Benoni Defense Black provokes white to advance a pawn from d4 to d5, with the idea of gaining control over the dark squares in the center.

Board 1

White's pawn advance secures an advantage in space.

Black's idea is that the advance of the white d-pawn has weakened white's control over d4 and e5.

The Benoni Defense is defined by the moves:
1 d4 ♞f6 **2** c4 c5 **3** d5 e6.

Black will try to advance on the queenside and dislodge the knight from c3. This will weaken white's defense of the e4 and d5 pawns.

White will try to play e4-e5 at some point and increase the advantage in space.

A typical continuation would be:
4 ♞c3 exd5 **5** cxd5 d6 **6** ♞f3 g6
7 e4 ♝g7 **8** ♝e2 0–0.

Board 2

Dutch Defense Black immediately establishes an asymmetrical
game. It is often difficult for both sides to play these positions correctly.

This move, followed by
♞g8–f6, is designed to
discourage white from
playing e2–e4.

Board 1

Black plays the Dutch Defense: **1** d4 f5.

Board 2

There is a sharp
struggle for the center
in this line of play,
which is called the
Leningrad Variation.
The pawn on d6 is weak,
but black has active
piece play.

The Leningrad Variation might continue like this:
2 g3 ♞f6 **3** ♝g2 g6 **4** ♞f3 ♝g7 **5** 0–0 0–0 **6** c4 d6
7 ♞c3 c6 **8** d5 e5 **9** dxe6 e.p. ♝xe6 **10** b3 ♞a6.

Flank Openings

The term *flank opening* is used to describe an opening system, which makes no immediate attempt to occupy the center with pawns. White plays to control the center with pieces. White will usually try to undermine any black attempt to occupy the center.

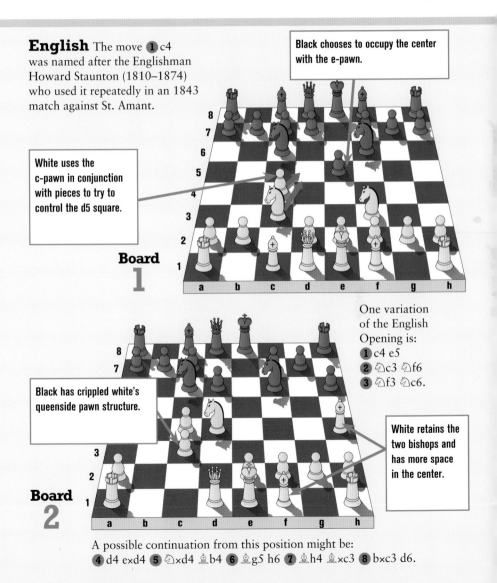

English The move ❶ c4 was named after the Englishman Howard Staunton (1810–1874) who used it repeatedly in an 1843 match against St. Amant.

Black chooses to occupy the center with the e-pawn.

White uses the c-pawn in conjunction with pieces to try to control the d5 square.

Board 1

One variation of the English Opening is:
❶ c4 e5
❷ ♘c3 ♘f6
❸ ♘f3 ♘c6.

Black has crippled white's queenside pawn structure.

White retains the two bishops and has more space in the center.

Board 2

A possible continuation from this position might be:
❹ d4 exd4 ❺ ♘xd4 ♗b4 ❻ ♗g5 h6 ❼ ♗h4 ♗xc3 ❽ bxc3 d6.

Réti Opening Named after Richard Réti (1889–1929) it appeared regularly in the 1920s and features the opening moves c4 and ♘f3 in either order.

The first move of the Réti Opening discourages black from playing ➊ ... e5.

White uses a wing pawn to attack black's center.

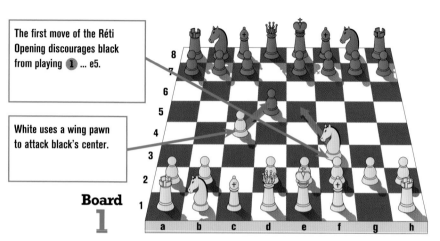

Board 1

The Réti Opening begins with:
➊ ♘f3 d5 ➋ c4.

Black seeks to secure control over d5 and e4.

White tries to control the center from a distance.

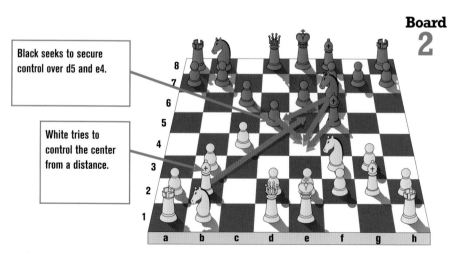

Board 2

A possible continuation might be:
➋ ... c6 ➌ b3 ♘f6 ➍ g3 ♗f5 ➎ ♗g2 e6 ➏ ♗b2.

Mastery Challenges III

☛ For answers, see pp.90 and 91

"I don't believe in psychology. I believe in good moves."

Bobby Fischer (1943–2008)

1 **The big four**
What are the four kinds of chess openings you learned about in this chapter?

2 **Match them up**
Match each of the boards below with one of the four kinds of chess openings you've named above.

Board
A

Board
B

Board
C

Board
D

Board
E

Board
F

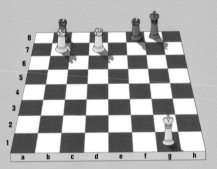

❸ Look ahead! Checkmate in three

In the play here, it's white to move. Can you find the checkmate in three moves?

In the next section, you'll learn important checkmate patterns. Remember, checkmate is the goal of chess. Everything else is simply a means of getting to that goal. So knowing these patterns is an essential game-winning skill.

ANSWERS

❶ **Open, semi-open, closed, and flank openings.** The opening is the first stage of a chess game. During this stage, a good player makes one or two pawn moves and gets his pieces off the back rank, effectively placed for the coming battle. Beyond the opening are the middlegame and the endgame. You'll learn about these stages in the coming sections.

2 **Board A is an open game.** Open games are characterized by 1. e4 e5. A is an early stage of the Philidor Defense—1. e4 e5 2. Nf3 d6. Black defends his e-pawn with his d-pawn while opening a diagonal for his light-square bishop. Now unfashionably stodgy, the Philidor remains a reasonable defense.

D and E are semi-open games. Semi-open games also begin with 1. e4, but then black replies with something other than 1. ... e5. D is the Advance Variation of the French Defense: 1. e4 e6 2. d4 d5 3. e5. White hopes his advanced pawn will cramp black's development. E is the very popular Sicilian Defense: 1. e4 c5. Both sides have lots of different plans after these initial pawn moves, but the die has been cast for imbalance and counterplay.

B and F are closed games. Nearly any game that begins with 1. d4 becomes a closed game, requiring maneuvering more than the wide-open cut-and-thrust, at least for some time. Players of white whose style leans toward postponing decisive tactics often choose closed games. B hasn't as yet defined the opening; more moves are necessary before we know exactly what to call it, but it will be one of the openings within the closed games. In F, the game began 1. d4 d5 2. c4 Nc6. It's called *Chigorin's Defense*. It's a difficult line to play because black blocks his own c-pawn. That pawn's advance is often a key to counterplay in the closed games.

C is a flank game. When white chooses not to occupy the center with a pawn in the first few moves, he's played a flank (side) opening. C illustrates the fancifully named *Orangutan Opening*. During the great New York 1924 tournament, Grandmaster Savielly Tartakower visited the Bronx Zoo, where he was impressed with an orangutan named Susan. In his game the next day, Tartakower played 1. b4 and dedicated the game to Susan. You'll also see this unusual opening referred to as the *Polish* or *Sokolsky Opening*.

3 1. Rg7+ Kh8 2. Rh8+ Kg8 3. R(b7)-g7#
This is an example of checkmate by force—there's nothing black can do to prevent his demise. Notice that the third move had to specify which rook was moving to g7, because either rook could go there. Only the rook on b7 could deliver checkmate, however. Look how in the final position black's own rook on f8 prevents his king's escape.

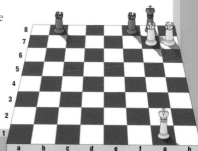

Section 4: MATING PATTERNS

Even though the number of possible chess moves is unimaginably large, there are certain patterns that recur too often to be a product of chance. The ability to recognize these patterns is one of the hallmarks of a good player. It is especially important to recognize mating patterns since they result in checkmate.

Back Rank Mates The most common mating pattern is referred to as the *back rank mate*. This type of mate occurs so frequently because castling is such a common occurrence. The king is simultaneously protected by a phalanx of pawns and trapped behind them.

Here the rook checks the king, which has no escape.

In this position, the black knight, rook, and queen are all incapable of defending the king from check.

A back rank mate can be delivered by either a rook or a queen.

These pawns block the king's escape route.

A back rank mate is not always the pawns' fault. Any friendly piece that blocks an escape route might be a culprit.

Board 1

Board 2

Smothered Mate The smothered mate is another example of a king's guardians being too close for comfort. The classic smothered mate involves a queen sacrifice followed by a fatal knight check.

The king is in check and must move to h8, because
1 ... ♔f8 is met by
2 ♕f7#.

Board 1

The above position is a typical example of how a smothered mate arises.

The king is smothered by its own defenders and is checkmated by the knight.

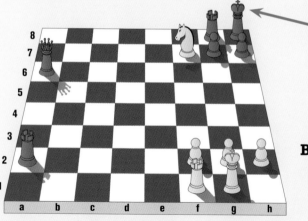

Board 2

Play continues with the following sequence of moves:
1 ... ♔h8 **2** ♘f7+ ♔g8 **3** ♘h6++ ♔h8 **4** ♕g8+ ♖xg8 **5** ♘f7#.
All of black's moves are forced—there are no alternatives and checkmate is unavoidable.

Queen and Pawn Mates

No piece, not even the powerful queen, can deliver checkmate by itself. The queen needs help, but just a little bit goes a long way.

The pawn attacks the g7 square, allowing white to play ① ♛g7#.

Board 1

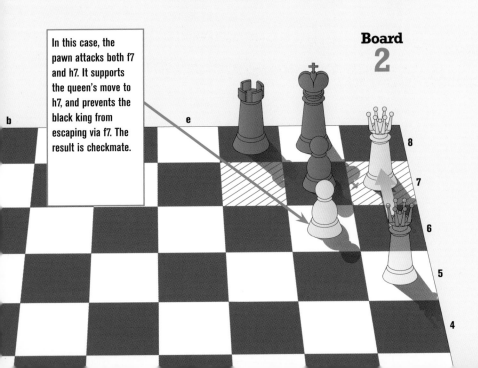

In this case, the pawn attacks both f7 and h7. It supports the queen's move to h7, and prevents the black king from escaping via f7. The result is checkmate.

Board 2

Damiano's Mate A Portuguese apothecary named Damiano published this position back in 1512.

Board 1

The presence of the pawn on g6 tells us that a queen move to h7 would deliver checkmate. However, the queen cannot move there directly, and **1** ♖h7 would not even be check, let alone checkmate. Damiano showed how to get the rooks out of the queen's way.

This is typical of the kind of position that leads to Damiano's mate.

The rooks were sacrificed to achieve the familiar queen and pawn mating pattern. Such sacrifices are often called *clearance sacrifices* (☛ see also p.130).

Here is Damiano's method:
1 ♖h8+ ♔xh8 **2** ♖h1+ ♔g8 **3** ♖h8+ ♔xh8
4 ♕h1+ ♔g8 **5** ♕h7#.

Board 2

Queen and Knight Mate The queen and knight

can combine in many ways to deliver checkmate. A typical
pattern involves a combined attack against a castled king.

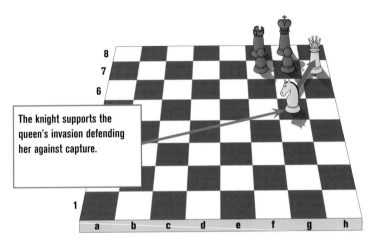

The knight supports the
queen's invasion defending
her against capture.

Example 1: This is the most common queen and
knight mate.

Example 2: This position is another
typical queen and knight mate.

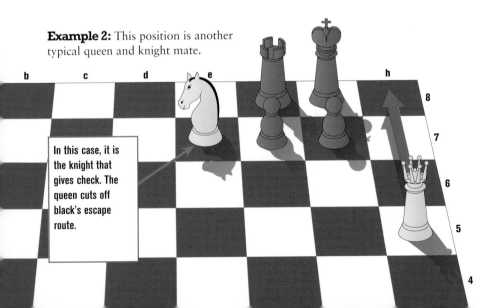

In this case, it is
the knight that
gives check. The
queen cuts off
black's escape
route.

Queen and Bishop Mates This battery is most effective when the queen is in front of the bishop.

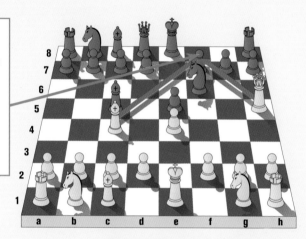

Sometimes called the *scholar's mate*, the white bishop and queen combine to attack f7, the weakest point in black's position. The queen delivers checkmate by capturing the pawn on f7.

Board 1

Example 1: Beginners often fall into a trap by playing the following game:
1 e4 e5 **2** ♗c4 ♗c5 **3** ♕h5 ♘f6.

The key to recognizing this pattern is to notice that when the bishop moves, the king will be checked by the white queen. You can use this free move to rearrange the position of the queen and bishop.

Example 2: Here is another common pattern.

Board 2

The bishop retreats to a square that cuts off black's escape route via f7.

White gives checkmate with the following sequence:
1 ♗g6+ ♔g8 **2** ♕h7#.

Rook and Rook It is important to be familiar with a mating pattern involving rooks on the 7th rank.

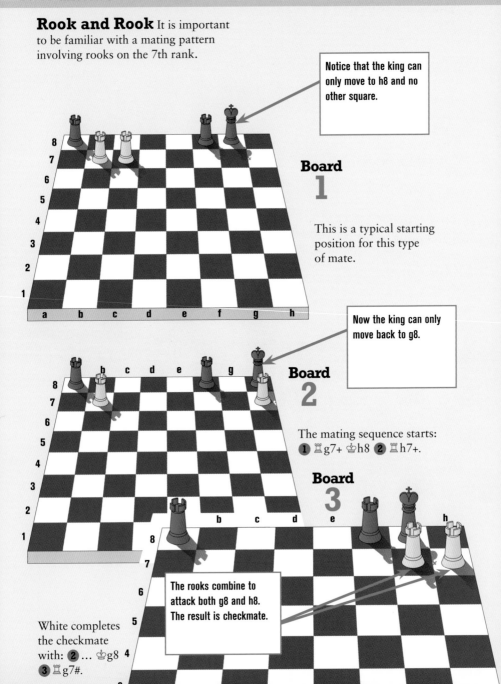

Notice that the king can only move to h8 and no other square.

Board 1

This is a typical starting position for this type of mate.

Now the king can only move back to g8.

Board 2

The mating sequence starts:
1 ♖g7+ ♔h8 **2** ♖h7+.

Board 3

The rooks combine to attack both g8 and h8. The result is checkmate.

White completes the checkmate with: **2** ... ♔g8 **3** ♖g7#.

Rook and Bishop
This mating pattern was demonstrated by the American champion Paul Morphy (1837–1884).

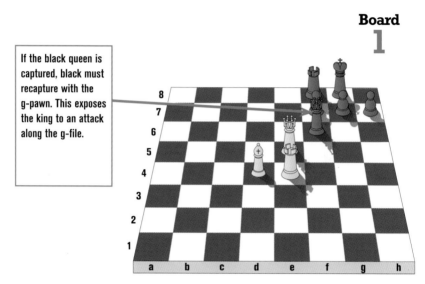

If the black queen is captured, black must recapture with the g-pawn. This exposes the king to an attack along the g-file.

This pattern leads to a typical rook and bishop mate.

The mating sequence is:
1 ♕×f6 g×f6 **2** ♖g4+ ♔h8 **3** ♗×f6#.

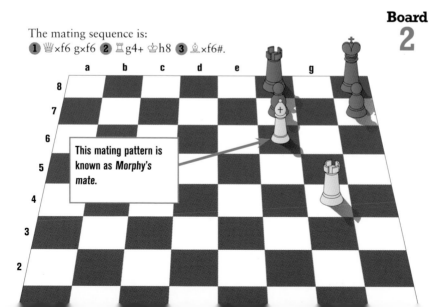

This mating pattern is known as *Morphy's mate.*

Rook and Knight

Rook and Knight The rook and knight usually need a little extra help in order to deliver checkmate. One example was provided in an 1803 novel by W. Heinse entitled *Anastasia and Chess*. The mating pattern is now known as *Anastasia's mate*.

The king has castled, but has only one escape square.

Board 1

Pattern 1 This position sets up Anastasia's mate.

The knight will check the king and force it to h8.

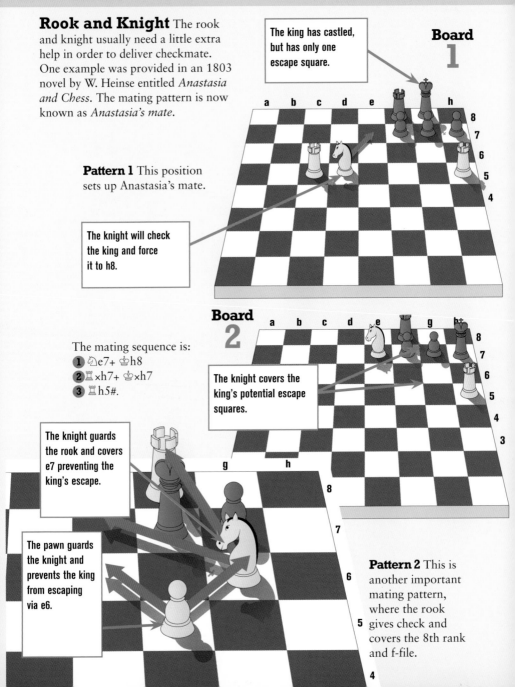

The mating sequence is:
1. ♘e7+ ♚h8
2. ♖xh7+ ♚xh7
3. ♖h5#.

Board 2

The knight covers the king's potential escape squares.

The knight guards the rook and covers e7 preventing the king's escape.

The pawn guards the knight and prevents the king from escaping via e6.

Pattern 2 This is another important mating pattern, where the rook gives check and covers the 8th rank and f-file.

Legall's Mate

Legall de Kermeur (1702–1792) was Philidor's teacher, but is most often remembered for the following mating pattern, which occurred in one of his games in 1750.

Board 1

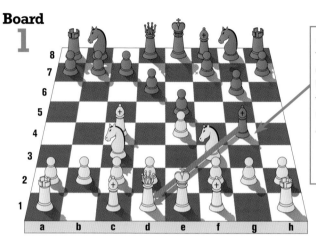

Black undoubtedly thought that the knight on f3 couldn't move, because it is pinned to the queen. White's next move must have come as a shock.

The game begins: **1** e4 e5 **2** ♘f3 d6 **3** ♗c4 ♗g4 **4** ♘c3 g6.

The knight delivers check and also cuts off black's remaining escape square on f6.

This knight does double duty by protecting the bishop on f7 and preventing the king's escape via d7.

Board 2

White wins by playing: **5** ♘xe5! ♗xd1? **6** ♗xf7+ ♔e7 **7** ♘d5#. Black could avoid being checkmated by not taking the white queen.

Greco's Mate

Greco's mate combines an attack on the f7 square with a mating threat on h7, and also involves a sacrifice.

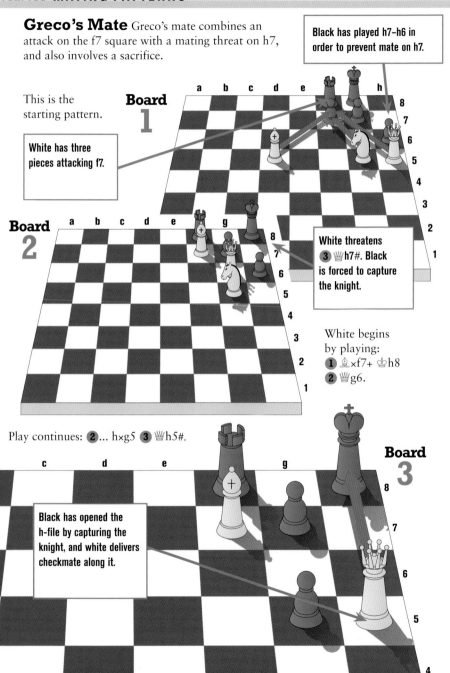

Black has played h7–h6 in order to prevent mate on h7.

This is the starting pattern.

Board 1

White has three pieces attacking f7.

Board 2

White threatens
3 ♕h7#. Black is forced to capture the knight.

White begins by playing:
1 ♗×f7+ ♔h8
2 ♕g6.

Play continues: 2... h×g5 3 ♕h5#.

Board 3

Black has opened the h-file by capturing the knight, and white delivers checkmate along it.

Boden's Mate

This mating pattern occurred in the game Schulder–Boden, London, early 1850s.

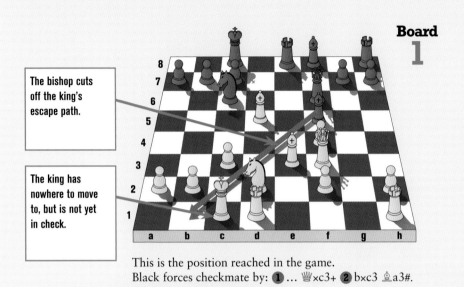

The bishop cuts off the king's escape path.

The king has nowhere to move to, but is not yet in check.

This is the position reached in the game.
Black forces checkmate by: **1** ... ♛×c3+ **2** b×c3 ♝a3#.

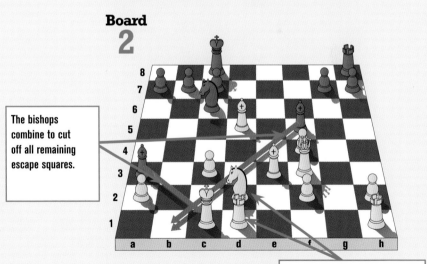

The bishops combine to cut off all remaining escape squares.

Notice how white's own pieces block the king's path.

Mastery Challenges IV

☞ For answers, see p.107

"Chess is imagination."

David Bronstein (1924–2006)

1 **Mate in One**
Exercise your checkmate muscle: Mate in one (or any number of moves) means that one side can force checkmate in the specified number of moves against the best defense. In each of the boards below, find the one-move checkmate.

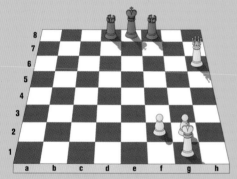

A. White to move

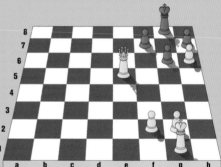

B. White to move

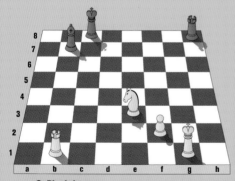

C. Black to move

D. White to move

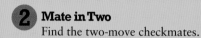

2 Mate in Two

Find the two-move checkmates.

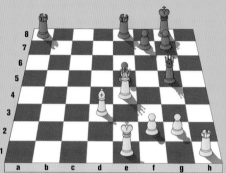

A. White to move

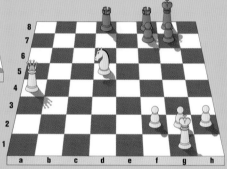

B. White to move

C. Black to move

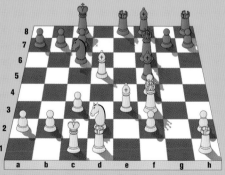

D. Black to move

3 **Mate in Three**
Find the three-moves checkmates.

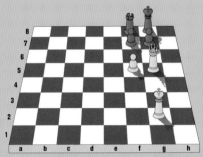

A. White to move

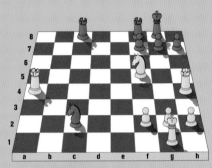

B. White to move

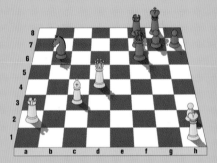

C. White to move

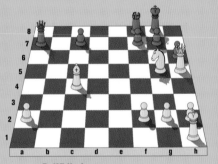

D. White to move

4 **The Captivating Smothered Checkmate**

Many chess devotees find the smothered checkmate to be the most beautiful checkmate of all. Thousands of players dream of the moment when they may have the opportunity to deliver the move in a real chess game. I once saw a player overlook the opportunity in his very first tournament game—what a tragedy! White to move: Show that you are prepared to deliver this checkmate.

ANSWERS

1 **A. Qe6#:** Congratulations if you found this one. It's a pattern, called the *epaulette mate*, not discussed in this chapter. Always be on the lookout for new ways to checkmate.
B. 1. Qg7#: A queen and pawn mate.
C. 1. ... Rh1#: A rook and bishop mate.
D. 1. Nh6#: A knight and bishop mate.

2 **A. 1. Rh8+! Kxh8 2. Qh7#:** A rook sacrifice to set up the queen-and-bishop battery mate. A "battery" is any two friendly long-range pieces—queens, rooks, bishops—lined up to support each other along a line of attack.
B. 1. Ne7+ Kh7 (or ... Kh8) 2. Qh4#: A queen and knight mate.
C. 1. ... Bg3+ 2. Kg1 Qh2#: Damiano's mate with queen and bishop rather than queen and pawn.
D. 1. ... Qxc3+ 2. bxc3 Ba3#: Boden's mate.

3 **A. 1. f6! g6 2. Qh6 (any move) 3. Qg7#:** Of course black couldn't play 1. ... gxf6 because it would expose his king to check.
B. 1. Ne7+ Kh8 2. Rxh7+ Kxh7 3. Rh4#: A clever rook sacrifice leading to a rook and knight mate.
C. 1. Qxf6 gxf6 2. Rg2+ Kh8 3. Bxf6#: Morphy's mate.
**D. 1. Bxf7+ Kh8 (if 1. ... Rxh7, 2. Qxf7+ Kh8 3. Qe8#) 2. Qg6 (threatening 3. Qh7#) hxg6
3. Qh5#: Greco's mate.

4 **1. Nf7+ Kg8 2. Nh6+ (a discovered double check) Kh8 (if 2. ... Kf8, then 3. Qf7#) 3. Qg8! Rxg7 4. Nf7#.** Note that black couldn't have played 3. ... Kxg7 because white's knight on h6 protects his queen. The sole remaining white piece checkmates the black king, who is suffocated by his own powerful rook.

Section 5: CENTER AND WING CONFIGURATIONS

In classical theory, action on the wings was delayed until securing the center. Nowadays, there are plausible exceptions to that rule.

The Center

The squares of a chessboard are all the same size and shape, but not of equal importance. The central squares are more important than the squares on the wing. Many chess games revolve around the struggle to control the four central squares. Controlling the center means more room to maneuver the pieces. If you lack control of the center, you will find your options more limited.

Open Center When the center is not blocked by pawns, it is referred to as an open center.

These are the most important squares on a chessboard.

The early pawn exchanges have brought the knights to the center of the board, where they are the most powerful.

The absence of three of the four center pawns ensures that the bishops will have excellent mobility.

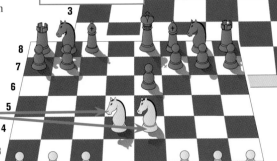

This opening leads to an open center:
1 d4 e6 **2** ♘f3 c5 **3** ♘c3 d5 **4** e4 dxe4
5 ♘xe4 cxd4 **6** ♕xd4 ♕xd4 **7** ♘xd4.

Closed Center

A closed center means that pawns are blocking the files and diagonals. The pieces will have difficulty maneuvering.

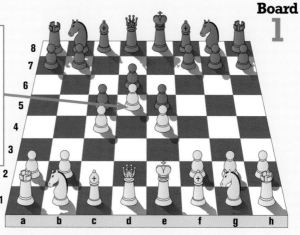

White can no longer exchange the d-pawn for either black's c- or e-pawn. The center has become locked, and can only be pried open with difficulty.

The following moves lead to a closed center:
1 d4 c5 **2** d5 d6 **3** c4 e5 **4** e4.

Closed centers are usually attacked by wing pawns.

Black will try to weaken white's pawn center by undermining the supporting pawns.

Both sides will try to weaken the other's position in the center.

Partially Blocked Center

The center is considered partially blocked if some lines are open and others closed.

White's pieces can occupy this square, but black pieces should not.

Pieces cannot occupy this square as long as the pawn remains there. The pawn also discourages black's pieces from moving to e5.

This variation of the French Defense leads to a partially blocked center:
1 d4 d5 **2** c4 e6 **3** ♘c3 ♘f6 **4** cxd5 exd5.

The c1–h6 and h2–b8 diagonals are open for this bishop, but the a1–h8 and g1–a7 diagonals are closed.

Tension In The Center

When both sides pass on the opportunity to exchange pawns in the center, they are said to be maintaining tension in the center.

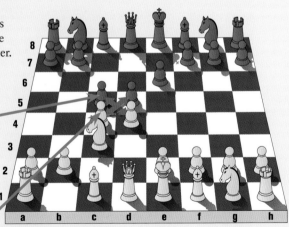

It is usually desirable to trade wing pawns for center pawns. The pawn exchange would relieve some of the tension in the center.

This pawn may capture the black d-pawn, or it may be captured in return. The tension between the pawns is maintained as long as captures are avoided.

While pawn captures in the center are possible, the nature of the center is unclear, and there is said to be tension. This opening is an example:
1 d4 d5 **2** c4 e6 **3** ♘c3 c5.

Classical Center

The classical view of the center advocated the use of pawns to occupy the center. The objective of many openings of that day was to establish a pawn duo on d4 and e4.

White has sacrificed some time in order to establish the pawn duo on e4 and d4. White would like to use these pawns to drive the black pieces away from the center.

In this opening, white places two pawns in the center:
1 e4 e5 **2** ♘f3 ♘c6 **3** ♗c4 ♗c5 **4** c3 ♘f6 **5** d4 exd4 **6** cxd4.

Little Center

The little (or small) center occurs when an exchange of one pair of center pawns results in an imbalance in the remaining ones. One pawn is more advanced than the other.

The black pawn's reach does not extend into white's territory.

The pawn on e4 is attacking squares in black's territory.

This is the typical pawn structure of the little center.

Piece Pressure A major part of the hypermodern revolution against classical dogma was the realization that occupation of the center did not guarantee control. One of the founders of the hypermodern school was Richard Réti (1889–1929).

The following position occurred in the game Réti–Yates, New York 1924.

Board 1

Black has established the classical center.

This was a revolutionary deployment of the queen. She is as far from centralized as possible, but still influences the center. The queen, bishop on b2, and knight on f3 all attack the pawn on e5.

This position was reached at the end of the opening.

Board 2

Bird's Opening attempts to control the dark center squares with a combination of pieces and pawns. White uses pawns not to occupy the center, but to attack it.

The fianchetto is now commonplace. The bishop attacks the center from long range, but is itself difficult to attack in return.

Here is another example:
1 f4 d5 **2** ♘f3 c5 **3** e3 ♘c6 **4** b3 ♘f6 **5** ♗b2 e6.

The Wings

Noncentral squares belong to the wings of the board. They are referred to as either the kingside or queenside. Classical theory dictated that the center must be secure before play on either wing could be justified. Modern theory is less dogmatic, and early play on the wings is no longer considered incorrect by definition.

Response In The Center

Flank attacks are often best met by a response in the center. Lev Alburt and Sam Palatnik give an excellent example of this principle in their book *Chess Strategy for the Tournament Player*. This position occurred in the game A. Rodriguez–Tringov, Buenos Aires 1978.

White has initiated an attack on the kingside by advancing the kingside pawns.

Board 1

This position was reached early in the middlegame.

The center has not been secured. The pawn move d6–d5 will break up the center, and white's exposed king will pay a heavy price.

White resigned, because there is no defense to ⑤ ... ♖d2. The action in the center opened lines that white wanted to keep closed.

The game continued:
① ... d5 ② ♔g2 dxe4
③ ♔h2 e3
④ ♗g2 ♖d8.

Board 2

Castling On The Same Wing

The status of the center usually determines whether pawn advances against the kings are advisable. In open or fluid cases, advancing pawns in front of your own king is usually far more weakening than threatening. If the center is closed, however, it is often safe for one side or the other. In the game Pilnik–Geller, Gothenburg 1955, black was in complete control.

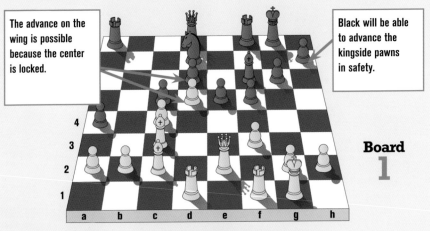

The advance on the wing is possible because the center is locked.

Black will be able to advance the kingside pawns in safety.

Board 1

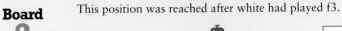

This position was reached after white had played f3.

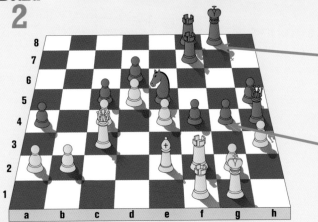

Board 2

Black's king is in no danger despite the advance of the kingside pawns.

Black will be able to force open lines against white's king. White resigned a few moves later.

The game continued: **1** ... e4 **2** ♗xf6 ♕xf6 **3** fxe4 f4 **4** ♖f2 ♘e5 **5** ♖df1 ♕h4 **6** ♗d1 ♖f7 **7** ♕c2 g5 **8** ♕c3 ♖af8 **9** h3 h5 **10** ♗e2 g4.

Castling On Opposite Wings

When kings have castled on opposite wings, players are generally free to advance pawns against them. These pawn storms occur on opposite sides of the board, and the race usually goes to the swiftest.

Since white has castled on the queenside, the kingside pawns can advance in relative safety. Both sides will try to use the pawns to pry open lines against the castled kings.

Board 1

Here is a typical opposite-wing castling position.

Pawn storms can be especially effective if the castled king position has been weakened. In this case the g-pawn is white's target. Black cannot prevent white from opening up the h-file.

Board 2

The advance of white's a-pawn has created a target for black.

Both sides advance pawns against the enemy king.

Mastery Challenges V

"If you have no center, your opponent has a freer position. If you do have a center, then you really have something to worry about!"

Siegbert Tarrasch (1862–1934)

1 **Chess matches**
To play chess well, you need to recognize different pawn configurations. Make the best match between each of the following terms and one of the boards below. Hint: You'll use each term once.

Closed Center
Classical Center
Wing Attack

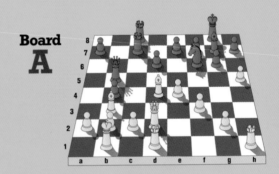

Board **A**

Board **B**

Board **C**

2 **Look ahead! Winning tactics**
In the next section, you'll learn the basic tools that win material. In this board, can you find a way for white to win the black piece?

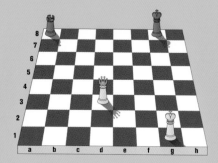

ANSWERS

1 **Closed Center = C.** The center is blocked and locked. The central pawns can't advance or capture each other.

Classical Center = B. White has the classical ideal. His center pawns occupy d4 and e4. His knight and bishop bear on the center.

Wing Attack = A. The opponents are castled on opposite sides and are storming each other's king positions with wing pawns. They know that the first to break through is most likely to win. The position is from a well-known game by the American Bobby Fischer, the most famous chess player of all time. Fischer became World Champion in 1972 by defeating Boris Spassky of the Soviet Union. For decades before this match, Soviet players had dominated the World Championship. A wonderful thing about chess: You can play over famous games from the past—and learn a lot from the comments of others! To play over this game online, just search for "Bobby Fischer–Bent Larsen, 1958."

2 White can play 1. Qd5+!. Notice that this move puts the queen on a square that attacks both the enemy king and the unprotected black rook. This is an example of the tactic we call the *fork* or *double attack*. Black has to move his king, and then the white queen gobbles up the rook, a win of major material.

Section 6: TACTICS

Chess is a game of strategy, but tactics factor into nearly every move. A tactic is a sequence of moves oriented toward a specific result, such as the win of material or checkmate.

Basic Tactics

There are certain tactical motifs that occur in almost every game. Others are more obscure, but are all the more powerful for their relative rarity. It's best to know as many tactics as possible, but it is essential to know the basics.

The Pin When a piece is attacked and cannot move without exposing a second, usually more valuable, piece to attack, it is said to be *pinned*. The queen, rook, and bishop are all capable of pinning pieces, but the knight and pawn are not. When the second piece is the king, it is called an *absolute pin*, because the pinned piece cannot move without exposing the king to check, which is not permitted by the laws of chess.

The rook is being pinned to the black king, and cannot move.

Example 1: Here is a simple pin.

This knight cannot move because it is pinned to the king.

Example 2: This diagram shows two more typical pins.

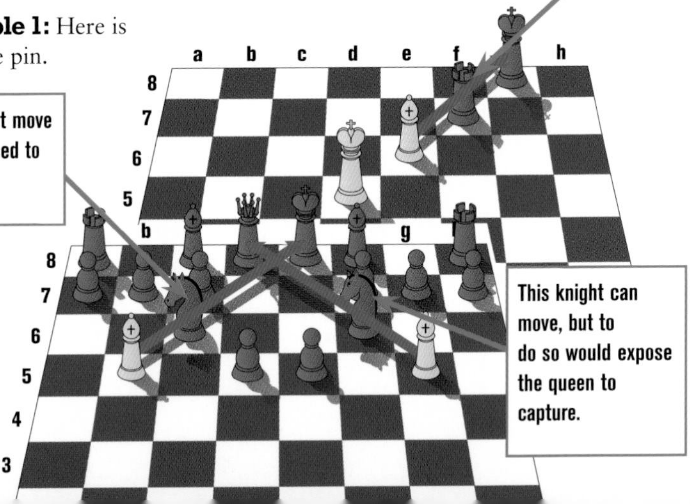

This knight can move, but to do so would expose the queen to capture.

Example 3: In this example, black escapes from a pin by making use of another pin.

The rook is pinned to the queen, but it is not an absolute pin.

Board 1

a b c d e f

8
7
6
5
4
3
2
1

The rook gives check, which must be responded to. White has no time to capture black's queen.

Board 2

a b c d e f

8
7
6
5
4
3
2
1

The bishop cannot capture the rook because it is now pinned to the king by the black queen.

Black plays
1 ... ♖f5+.

The bishop can capture the queen, but not the rook.

If the queen and king are on the same rank, file, or diagonal a pin is possible.

Example 4: Some more pins.

a b c d e f

8

The rook is pinning the queen to the king. However, the rook can simply be captured by the queen. Its apparent defender, the black queen, has been paralyzed by a pin.

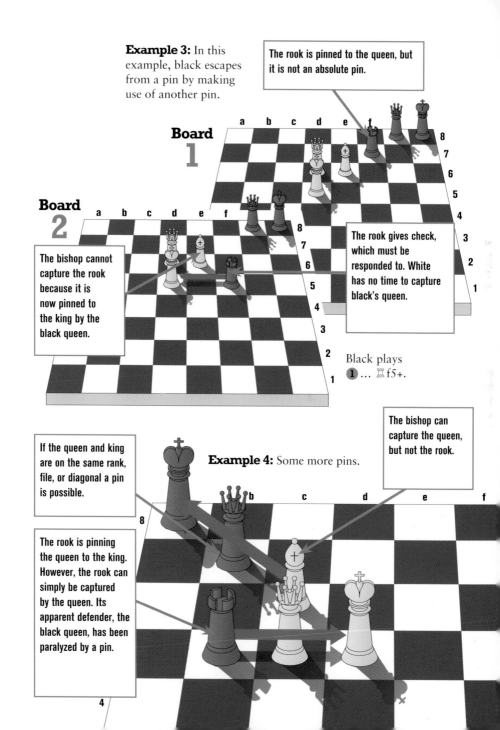

4

Forks A fork is a type of double attack. One piece attacks two simultaneously. Any piece can be used to fork others, but the knight fork is the most common.

White is threatening to play ⑨ ♘×d6+ followed by ⑩ ♕f7#. Black must move the queen in order to protect against this threat. That allows white to play a knight fork.

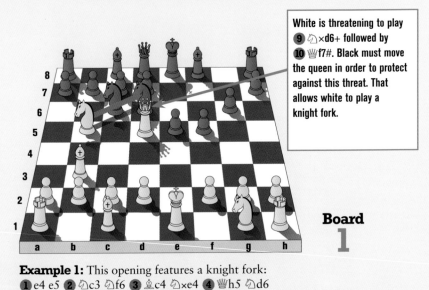

Board
1

Example 1: This opening features a knight fork:
① e4 e5 ② ♘c3 ♘f6 ③ ♗c4 ♘×e4 ④ ♕h5 ♘d6
⑤ ♗b3 ♘c6 ⑥ ♘b5 g6 ⑦ ♕f3 f5 ⑧ ♕d5.

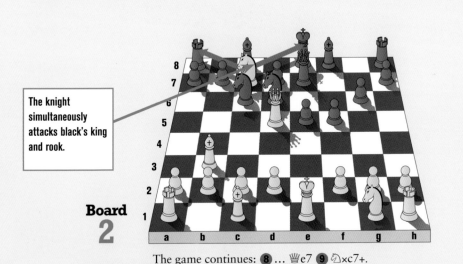

The knight simultaneously attacks black's king and rook.

Board
2

The game continues: ⑧ ... ♕e7 ⑨ ♘×c7+.

The pawn on d5 is forking white's bishop and knight. One of them must be lost.

White must respond to the queen's check. Whatever white does, black will take the bishop on g5 on the next move.

Example 2: Here is an example of a pawn fork: **1** e4 e5 **2** ♘c3 ♘f6 **3** ♗c4 ♘xe4 **4** ♘xe4 d5.

Example 3: This diagram shows a fork by the queen: **1** d4 ♘f6 **2** ♗g5 c6 **3** e3 ♕a5+.

The Skewer The term *skewer* was invented by a Liverpool schoolteacher, Edgar Pennell, in 1937. It describes an attack which forces one piece to move, exposing a second piece behind it to capture.

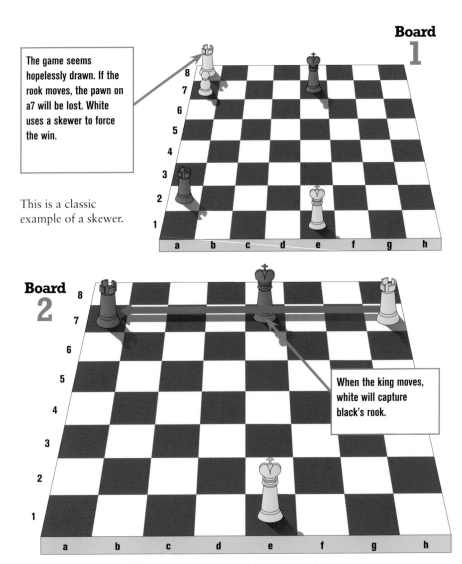

The game seems hopelessly drawn. If the rook moves, the pawn on a7 will be lost. White uses a skewer to force the win.

This is a classic example of a skewer.

Board 1

Board 2

When the king moves, white will capture black's rook.

White can win the game by using a skewer:
1 ♖h8 ♖×a7 **2** ♖h7+.

Double Attack

A double attack usually occurs when one move creates separate attacks by two different pieces.

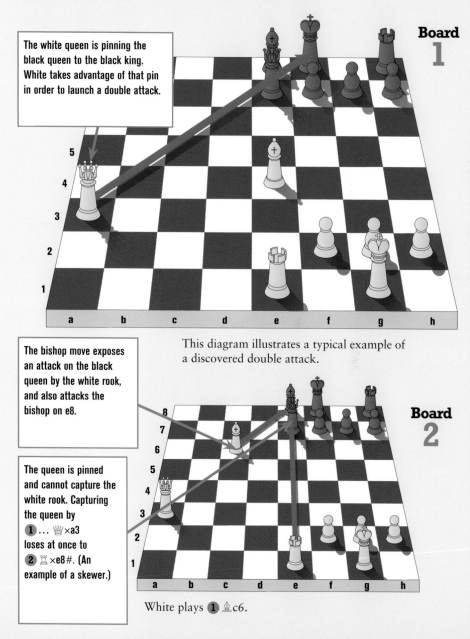

The white queen is pinning the black queen to the black king. White takes advantage of that pin in order to launch a double attack.

Board 1

This diagram illustrates a typical example of a discovered double attack.

The bishop move exposes an attack on the black queen by the white rook, and also attacks the bishop on e8.

Board 2

The queen is pinned and cannot capture the white rook. Capturing the queen by

1 ... ♛×a3

loses at once to

2 ♖×e8#. (An example of a skewer.)

White plays **1** ♗c6.

Discovered Check A discovered check occurs when the movement of one piece allows a second stationary piece to give check. This can be a very powerful maneuver, because the first piece can wreak havoc as the check must be dealt with.

Board 1

If this knight moves away from the attack by the white queen, white will be able to play a discovered check.

Petroff's Defense can lead to an early discovered check:
1 e4 e5 **2** ♘f3 ♘f6 **3** ♘xe5 ♘xe4 **4** ♕e2.

The c6 square looks off-limits to white's pieces because it is defended by the knight on b8 and the black b- and d-pawns. However, none of these potential captures is possible until black responds to the check from the queen.

The queen is lost. The knight will capture it on d8 (or e7 if the queen moves there in order to block the check).

Board 2

The knight was the piece that moved, but it is the queen that gives check.

If black retreats the knight, the following will happen:
4 ... ♘f6 **5** ♘c6+.

Double Check A double check occurs when a discovered check is combined with a second check by the moving piece. There is only one way to respond to a double check: the king is forced to move. The following position occurred in the game Réti–Tartakower, Vienna 1910, and features one of the most famous double checks in chess history. The final position is known as *Réti's mate*.

Board
1

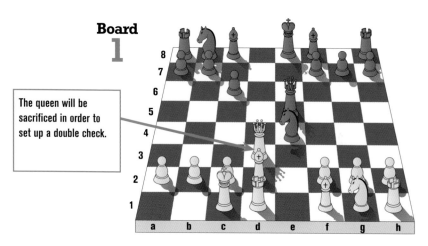

The queen will be sacrificed in order to set up a double check.

Black's knight has just captured a white knight on e4.

Board
2

The king is being checked by the rook on d1 and the bishop on g5. The king must move and has only a choice of poisons:
2 ... ♔c7 **3** ♗d8 # or
2 ... ♔e8 **3** ♖d8 #.
In the actual game he chose the former.

White responded with: **1** ♕d8+ ♔xd8 **2** ♗g5++.

Sacrifices

A sacrifice is an intentional loss of material. Sometimes a sacrifice is merely temporary. A stock sacrifice is one where the outcome is both favorable and familiar.

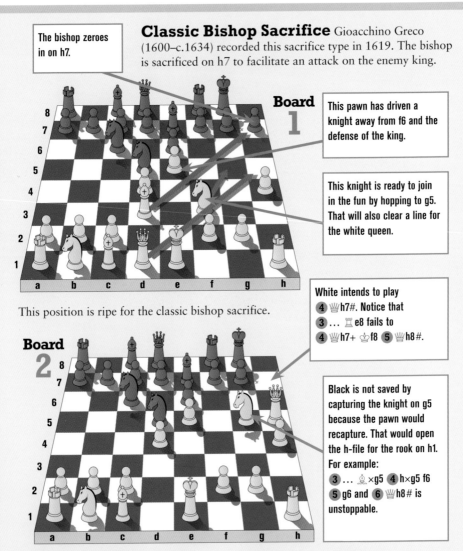

The bishop zeroes in on h7.

Classic Bishop Sacrifice Gioacchino Greco (1600–c.1634) recorded this sacrifice type in 1619. The bishop is sacrificed on h7 to facilitate an attack on the enemy king.

Board 1

This pawn has driven a knight away from f6 and the defense of the king.

This knight is ready to join in the fun by hopping to g5. That will also clear a line for the white queen.

This position is ripe for the classic bishop sacrifice.

White intends to play
4 ♕h7#. Notice that
3 ... ♖e8 fails to
4 ♕h7+ ♔f8 **5** ♕h8#.

Board 2

Black is not saved by capturing the knight on g5 because the pawn would recapture. That would open the h-file for the rook on h1. For example:
3 ... ♗×g5 **4** h×g5 f6
5 g6 and **6** ♕h8# is unstoppable.

White continues by playing **1** ♗×h7+ ♔×h7 **2** ♘g5+ ♔g8 **3** ♕h5.

Lasker's Sacrifice

Emanuel Lasker (1868–1941) played this sacrifice in a game from 1889. It is also known as the *Double Bishop sacrifice*.

Board 1

Black has captured a piece on h5 with his last move, and probably expected Lasker to play ♕×h5.

Instead, Lasker played

1 ♗×h7+ ♚×h7 **2** ♕×h5+ ♚g8 **3** ♗×g7 ♚×g7 **4** ♕g4+ ♚h7 **5** ♖f3.

This is the position that Lasker reached.

The bishops have robbed the king of his pawn cover.

White threatens

6 ♖h3#. Lasker went on to win after

5 ... e5 **6** ♖h3+ ♕h6 **7** ♖×h6+ ♚×h6 **8** ♕d7.

Board 2

Permanent Sacrifices A permanent sacrifice occurs when the goal is not to recover the material in the short run. It is usually made in order to secure a lasting strategic advantage. Many gambits involve permanent sacrifices. The Milner-Barry Gambit, a variation of the French Defense, is an example.

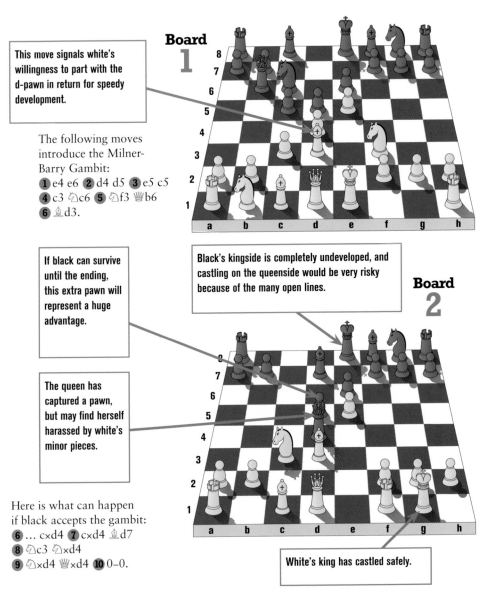

This move signals white's willingness to part with the d-pawn in return for speedy development.

The following moves introduce the Milner-Barry Gambit:
1 e4 e6 **2** d4 d5 **3** e5 c5
4 c3 ♘c6 **5** ♘f3 ♛b6
6 ♗d3.

Board 1

If black can survive until the ending, this extra pawn will represent a huge advantage.

The queen has captured a pawn, but may find herself harassed by white's minor pieces.

Black's kingside is completely undeveloped, and castling on the queenside would be very risky because of the many open lines.

Board 2

Here is what can happen if black accepts the gambit:
6 ... cxd4 **7** cxd4 ♗d7
8 ♘c3 ♘xd4
9 ♘xd4 ♛xd4 **10** 0-0.

White's king has castled safely.

Temporary Sacrifices

The temporary sacrifice expects immediate returns. There is always some means of regaining the lost material—often with dividends attached. One such temporary sacrifice occurred in the game Feliciano–Eade, 1980.

Board 1

Black has just sacrificed a knight for a pawn. The sacrifice is only temporary.

The game began:

1 e4 e6 **2** d4 d5 **3** ♘c3 ♘f6 **4** ♗g5 ♗b4 **5** e5 h6
6 ♗d2 ♗xc3 **7** ♗xc3 ♘e4 **8** ♗b4 c5 **9** dxc5 ♘xf2.

Board 2

The queen checked the white king from h4 and then captured the bishop on b4. What started as a sacrifice of knight for pawn has ended up as a trade of the knight for bishop and pawn. The temporary sacrifice has resulted in a net gain for black.

White has to take the knight, but black recovers the piece easily: **10** ♔xf2 ♕h4+ **11** g3 ♕xb4.

Clearance Sacrifices When your own pieces are preventing you from carrying out a winning maneuver, you might consider a clearance sacrifice. The piece that's gumming up the works is jettisoned overboard to make room for a more opportunistic one. Here's a position from Salov–Ehlvest, Skelleftea 1989.

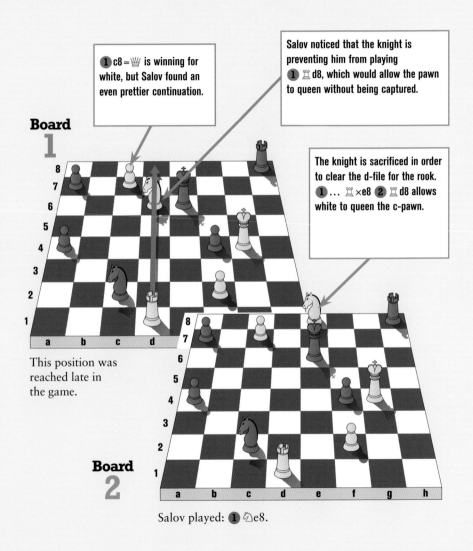

① c8 = ♕ is winning for white, but Salov found an even prettier continuation.

Salov noticed that the knight is preventing him from playing **①** ♖ d8, which would allow the pawn to queen without being captured.

The knight is sacrificed in order to clear the d-file for the rook. **①** ... ♖ ×e8 **②** ♖ d8 allows white to queen the c-pawn.

Board 1

This position was reached late in the game.

Board 2

Salov played: **①** ♘e8.

Queen Sacrifices Any piece may be sacrificed with the exception of the king. Queen sacrifices, however, are a special case, because the queen is so powerful. It takes quite a lot to make up for the absence of the queen. Although it is possible to sacrifice the queen in order to obtain other objectives, mate is the usual goal.

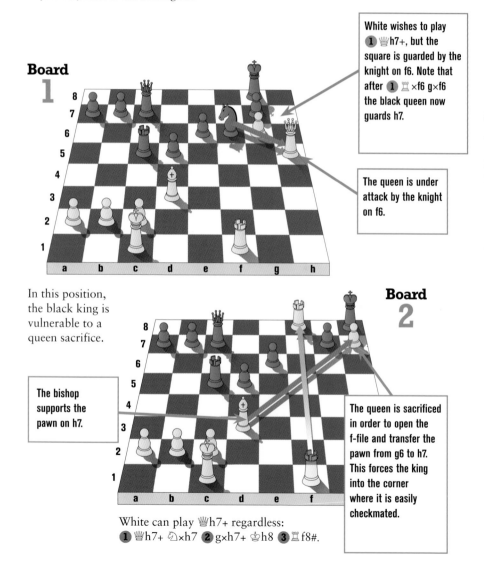

Board 1

White wishes to play **1** ♕h7+, but the square is guarded by the knight on f6. Note that after **1** ♖×f6 g×f6 the black queen now guards h7.

The queen is under attack by the knight on f6.

In this position, the black king is vulnerable to a queen sacrifice.

Board 2

The bishop supports the pawn on h7.

The queen is sacrificed in order to open the f-file and transfer the pawn from g6 to h7. This forces the king into the corner where it is easily checkmated.

White can play ♕h7+ regardless:
1 ♕h7+ ♘×h7 **2** g×h7+ ♚h8 **3** ♖f8#.

Combinations

A sequence of moves designed to carry out a specific objective is called a *combination*. Combinations usually rely on tactics in order to achieve the objective, and often contain sacrifices. There are many combinative themes that reoccur in chess. Every strong chess player has the ability to recognize these combinative patterns.

Deflection Deflection is a very common tactical theme. As the name suggests, deflection distracts a piece away from its primary responsibility.

This knight is defending the black queen and the g8 square. If it can be forced to move, the queen will be lost.

The check forces black to capture the rook with the knight. The black queen would be lost after

① ...♘×g8
② ♕×c6.

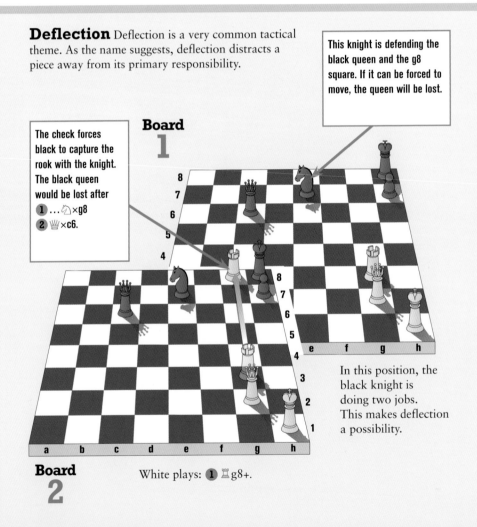

Board 1

Board 2

In this position, the black knight is doing two jobs. This makes deflection a possibility.

White plays: ① ♖g8+.

Destroying The Guard Sometimes a single piece is holding a position together. A sacrifice in order to capture that piece often pays dividends. The following example arose in the game Smyslov–Lilienthal, Moscow 1941.

The rook is attacking the queen and will capture white's rook if she simply retreats.

The black rook is defended by both these pieces.

Board 1

One of the rook's defenders has been destroyed.
1 ... ♕×d6 would remove the other and would lose to
2 ♖×e8+ followed by mate.

The queen is immune to capture.

Board 2

Black cannot capture the rook either, because of the back rank weakness:
1 ... ♖×e1
2 ♕f8 #.

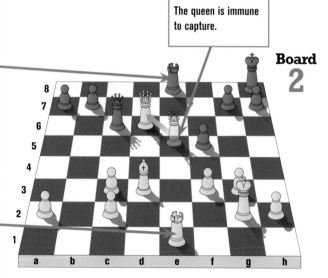

White wins by destroying the rook's guard: **1** ♕×d6.

Overloading A piece can sometimes bite off more than it can chew by doing too many things at once. You can exploit an overloaded piece by forcing it to abandon one responsibility in order to address another. Black overloaded a white piece in the game Drimer–Pomar, Leipzig 1960.

Board 1

In this diagram, black overloads the white rook.

Black has just played the rook to c1, even though it can be captured.

This rook is now overloaded. Its primary job is to defend against the threatened checkmate on g2, but it also has to protect the queen.

Board 2

The rook must capture the bishop, but in doing so will give up its defense of the queen.

White has to take the rook, since otherwise the bishop is lost: **1** ♕xc1 ♗xg2+.

Decoy

A decoy is used to lure a piece to a poisonous spot. The lure is usually a sacrifice that must be accepted.

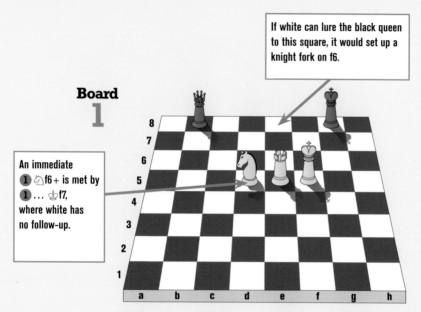

If white can lure the black queen to this square, it would set up a knight fork on f6.

An immediate
1 ♘f6 + is met by
1 ... ♔f7,
where white has no follow-up.

Board 1

White can use a decoy here to win the black queen.

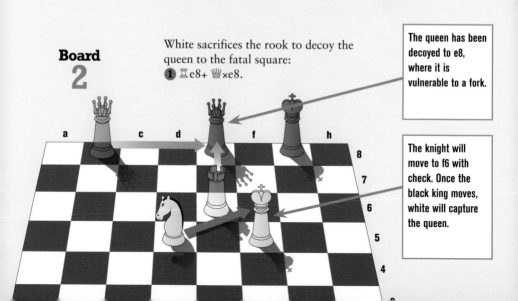

Board 2

White sacrifices the rook to decoy the queen to the fatal square:
1 ♖e8+ ♕xe8.

The queen has been decoyed to e8, where it is vulnerable to a fork.

The knight will move to f6 with check. Once the black king moves, white will capture the queen.

Interference

Interference occurs when you force your opponent's chessmen to block themselves. Pieces that were formerly cooperative turn into their own worst enemies.

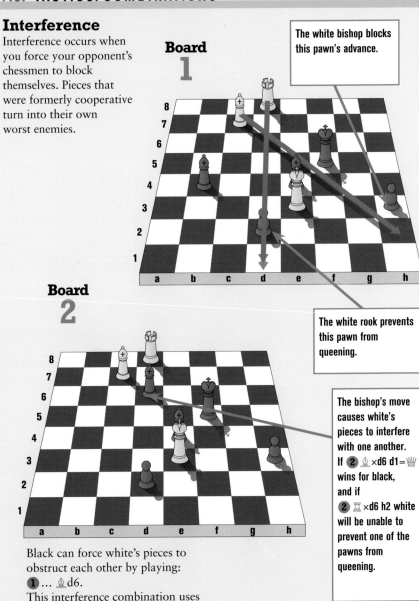

Board 1

The white bishop blocks this pawn's advance.

The white rook prevents this pawn from queening.

Board 2

The bishop's move causes white's pieces to interfere with one another. If **2** ♗×d6 d1=♛ wins for black, and if **2** ♖×d6 h2 white will be unable to prevent one of the pawns from queening.

Black can force white's pieces to obstruct each other by playing:
1 ... ♗d6.
This interference combination uses a bishop sacrifice.

Windmill The windmill (or see-saw) is a deadly combination of checks and discovered checks. A helpless king is forced to toggle between two squares while his army is demolished.

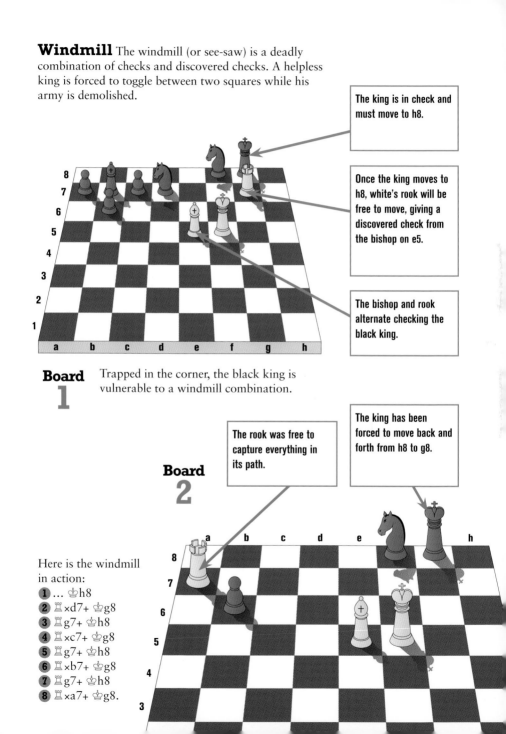

The king is in check and must move to h8.

Once the king moves to h8, white's rook will be free to move, giving a discovered check from the bishop on e5.

The bishop and rook alternate checking the black king.

Board 1 Trapped in the corner, the black king is vulnerable to a windmill combination.

The rook was free to capture everything in its path.

The king has been forced to move back and forth from h8 to g8.

Board 2

Here is the windmill in action:
1 ... ♚h8
2 ♖×d7+ ♚g8
3 ♖g7+ ♚h8
4 ♖×c7+ ♚g8
5 ♖g7+ ♚h8
6 ♖×b7+ ♚g8
7 ♖g7+ ♚h8
8 ♖×a7+ ♚g8.

X-ray The X-ray tactic exploits a player's control over a square which appears to be controlled by the opponent's pieces. It can be quite a shock to see a piece settle on a square you considered off-limits.

It may seem as though the black rook controls this square, but it is actually controlled by the white rook due to an X-ray attack.

If the rooks are traded, black would have a good game.

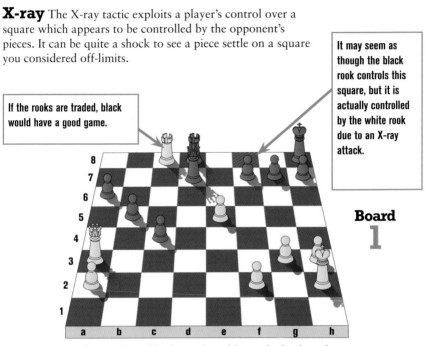

Board 1

In this position, black is vulnerable on the back rank.

The rook is forced to capture the queen, but is captured in return by the white rook:
1 ♕f8+ ♖×f8
2 ♖×f8#.

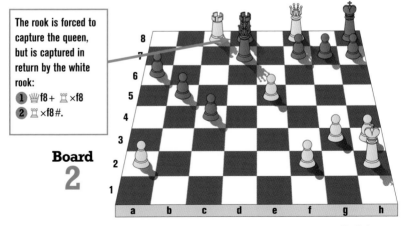

Board 2

White exploits the X-ray protection of f8 by 1 ♕f8+.

Zwischenzug A German word normally translated as an "in-between move." It is a move played instead of a seemingly forced one. The natural capture–recapture balance is disturbed, as in this example from Fischer–Byrne, New York 1965.

The bishop is now under attack from the knight on c6.

Fischer has just captured a knight on c6, and almost certainly expected Byrne to recapture with the b-pawn.

Board 1

In this position, Bobby Fischer overlooks a zwischenzug.

Board 2

The bishop move creates a mating threat on h2 (♛×h2#), which cannot be ignored.

The game continued **2** h3 ♗×e2, winning material and eventually the game.

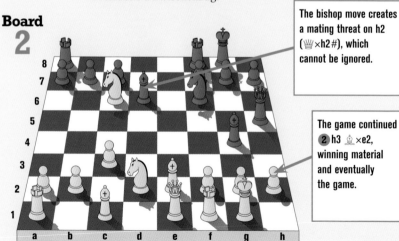

Byrne finds a zwischenzug that saves the bishop: **1** ... ♗d6.

Mastery Challenges VI

☞ For answers, see pp.142 and 143

"Chess is 99% tactics." Richard Teichmann (1868–1925)

1 Practice your tactics

In each board below, use the tactics you've learned to find the best move. We include some hints on the first page and at the end.

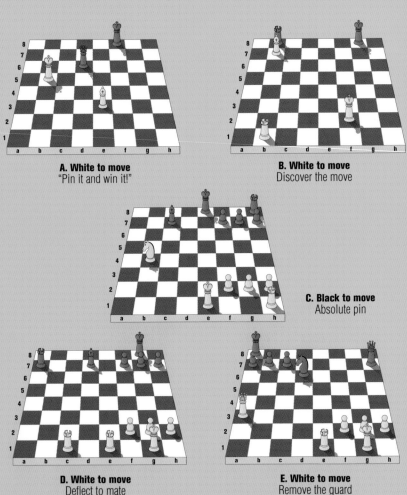

A. White to move
"Pin it and win it!"

B. White to move
Discover the move

C. Black to move
Absolute pin

D. White to move
Deflect to mate

E. White to move
Remove the guard

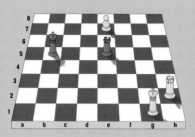

F. White to move

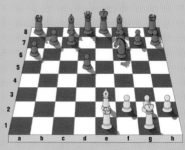

G. White to move

H. White to move

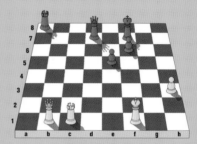

I. White to move

J. White to move

K. White to move

L. White to move
Take all the pieces on the 7th rank

M. White to move
Give one, get one!

2 Look ahead! Good and bad bishops

In addition to tactics (short-term actions) players must know strategy (long-term planning). Which one of the white bishops below is the stronger piece?

Board
A

Board
B

ANSWERS

1 **A:** 1. Bc5!, *pinning* the black queen to her king. The best black then has is **1. ... Qxc5+**, when white plays **2. Kxc5**, and the game is a draw. Without this tactic, black would win easily with queen against bishop.

B: 1. Bd5!, *discovering check* on the king and a simultaneous attack on the black rook. Black must move his king and lose the rook to **2. Rxb8**.

C: 1. ... Ba5 *pins* the knight to the king. The knight can't be supported in time, so black will simply capture it next move.

D: 1. Rc8+!. Black must capture on c8 with his bishop, which is thus *deflected* from the defense of e8: **1. ... Bxc8 2. Re8#**.

E: 1. Qxd6! wins the knight and *removes the guard* on e8. If black recaptures, white plays **2. Re8#**.

F: 1. Rh5!. Black's rook is *pinned* to his king, so he might as well play 1. ... Rxh5, but then 2. e8(Q)+ queens the pawn with a fork on black's two pieces. This little *combination* is a beautiful example of tactics working together: *pin, sacrifice, deflection, decoy,* and, finally, *double attack*! So much happening on a board holding only four pieces!

G: 1. Bb5!#. The black king can't get out of both checks in one move.

H: 1. Re1!. White *pins* black's valuable queen to his king, winning the queen for a rook. You'll win many queens this way!

I: 1. Rc7! Qxc7 2. Qh7+. *Decoy*! White sacrifices his rook to move the black queen one square farther away from her king in order to *skewer* it. To see why the rook sacrifice was necessary, look at the effects of 1. Qh7+? Ke6.

J: 1. e7!+. *Discovered check*—the nuclear bomb of chess! Black must move his king, when white will play 2. exd8(Q)!.

K: 1. Bb6!. A *clearance idea* from the game Benko-Fuester, 1958. The bishop attacks the valuable queen while getting out of the way of the now-threatened 2. Qh6!#. Black can't defend against both threats at once.

L: 1. Rxf7+ (*discovered check*) 1. . ... Kg8 (the only legal move) 2. Rg7+ Kh8 3. Rxe7+ Kg8 4. Rg7+ Kh8 5. Rxd7—rinse and repeat, until all the black pieces on the 7th rank have been captured. This is the windmill combination.

M: 1. Qg1+!. A queen sacrifice that *decoys* the black queen so that she can be *skewered*. 1. ... Qxg1 (otherwise, black loses his queen immediately) 2. g8(Q)+, when black must move his king, and white plays 3. Qxg1.

2 B is the good bishop. The bishop in Board A is imprisoned by his own pawns and has almost no influence on the board.

Section 7: POSITIONAL CONSIDERATIONS

Factors that are more strategic in nature are often referred to as *positional considerations*. These are the building blocks of chess mastery.

Open Files If there are no pawns on a file, it is an open file. The easiest way to activate a rook is to create and control an open file.

Board 1

This rook has fewer squares to move to.

This rook is free to move along the entire d-file.

In this diagram, the white rook is on an open file.

The rook has used the d-file to successfully invade black's position.

This pawn is under attack. The defensive try ② ... b6 allows ③ ♖×a7, so white must win one pawn or the other.

White's rook enters black's territory along the open file: ① ♖d7 ♖b8 ② ♖c7.

Board 2

Doubled Rooks

The struggle for control over an open file has determined the course of many a game. One way to establish control is to put both rooks on the same file. This is called *doubling*.

Black's rooks can never contest the d-file, and are doomed to passivity.

White controls the only open file. The rooks are doubled on the d-file.

This diagram illustrates the idea of doubled rooks.

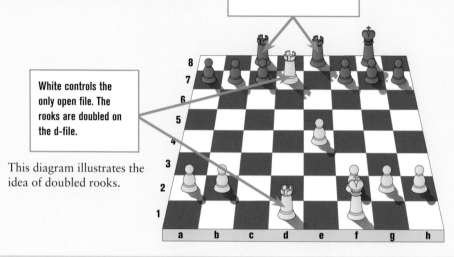

Tripling

When you add the queen to the same file as the doubled rooks, you get tripling.

The knight's future is grim. It cannot move or the rook on e8 will be lost.

The queen can be in front of, behind, or in between the rooks, and it is still called *tripling*.

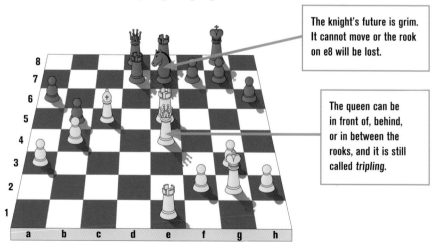

This diagram illustrates the power of tripled pieces.

The 7th Rank If your rooks can successfully invade the enemy position along the 7th rank, you will usually secure a significant advantage. Pawns that remain on their original squares become sitting ducks, and the king may often be trapped on the 8th rank and vulnerable to attack.

A rook on the 7th may attack pawns that have remained on their original squares.

Example 1: The white rook in this diagram dominates the 7th rank.

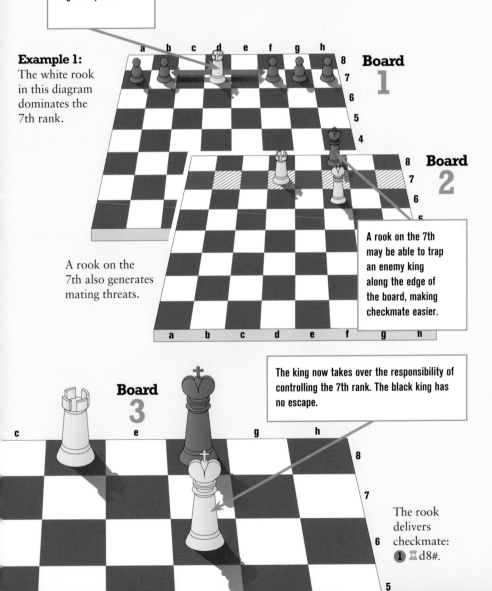

Board 1

Board 2

A rook on the 7th also generates mating threats.

A rook on the 7th may be able to trap an enemy king along the edge of the board, making checkmate easier.

Board 3

The king now takes over the responsibility of controlling the 7th rank. The black king has no escape.

The rook delivers checkmate: **1** ♖d8#.

Example 2: Doubled rooks on the 7th can be even more deadly. Whoever moves first in this position wins.

The doubled rooks allow white to move one of them away while still controlling the 7th rank.

Black threatens an immediate mate by either **1** ... ♖c1# or **1** ... ♖e1#. It is a bit more complicated if it is white's turn to move.

Board 1

In this diagram, both sides have managed to double their rooks on the 7th rank.

Board 2

White has traded one rook for two of black's. Doubled rooks on the 7th are no guarantee of victory, but they are very powerful indeed.

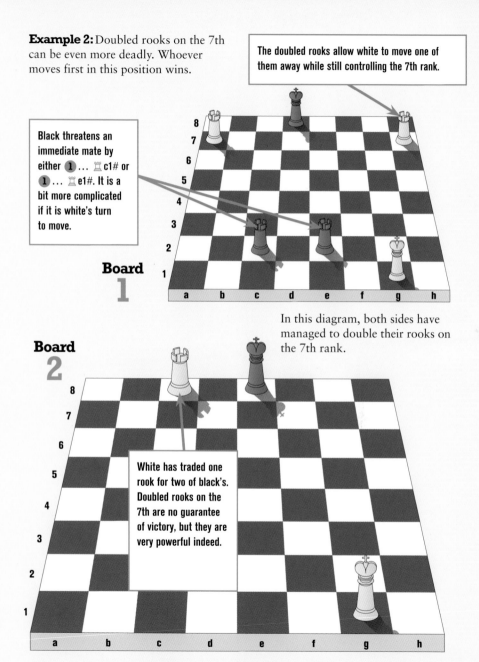

White can win by playing **1** ♖h8+ ♖e8 **2** ♖a8+ ♖c8 **3** ♖xe8+ ♔xe8 **4** ♖xc8+.

Luft The word *luft* is short for the German word *luftloch*, which translates as "airhole." In chess terms the word means escape square. It applies most commonly to the castled king. If there is any vulnerability to a back rank mate, creating luft by moving one of the pawns in front of the king is a wise precaution.

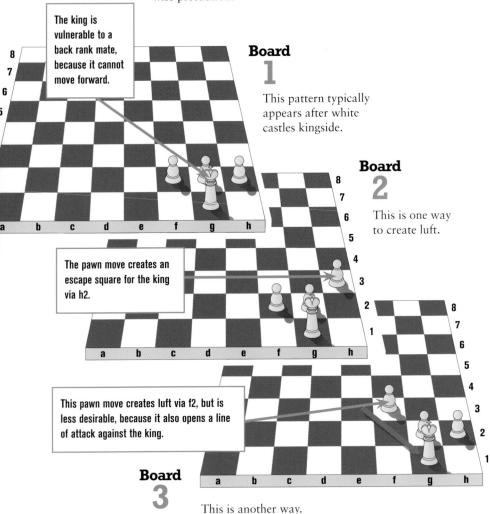

Board 1

The king is vulnerable to a back rank mate, because it cannot move forward.

This pattern typically appears after white castles kingside.

Board 2

This is one way to create luft.

The pawn move creates an escape square for the king via h2.

Board 3

This pawn move creates luft via f2, but is less desirable, because it also opens a line of attack against the king.

This is another way.

The Two Bishops If you have both your bishops, and your opponent does not, you are said to have the *advantage of the two bishops*. It must be pointed out that this advantage exists primarily in open positions. The value of the knights increases in closed positions, when the bishops' mobility decreases. However, it is easier to open a game than close it, and the two bishops represent an advantage more often than not.

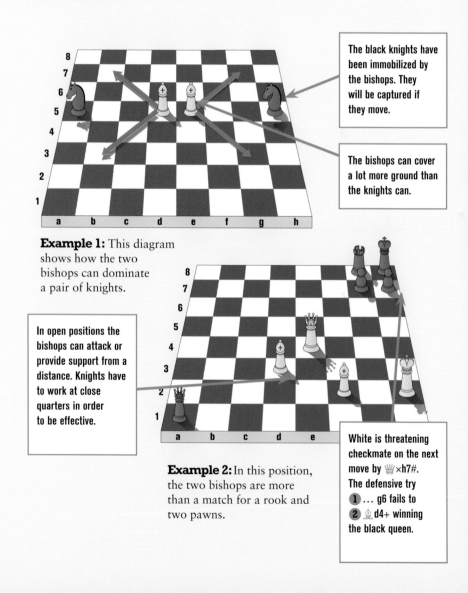

The black knights have been immobilized by the bishops. They will be captured if they move.

The bishops can cover a lot more ground than the knights can.

Example 1: This diagram shows how the two bishops can dominate a pair of knights.

In open positions the bishops can attack or provide support from a distance. Knights have to work at close quarters in order to be effective.

Example 2: In this position, the two bishops are more than a match for a rook and two pawns.

White is threatening checkmate on the next move by ♕×h7#. The defensive try **1** ... g6 fails to **2** ♗d4+ winning the black queen.

Blockade One of the knight's best attributes is its ability to blockade or prevent a pawn's advance. Pawns can only move forward and are unable to attack the square in front of them. If a pawn cannot move, it may hamper the mobility of the other pieces.

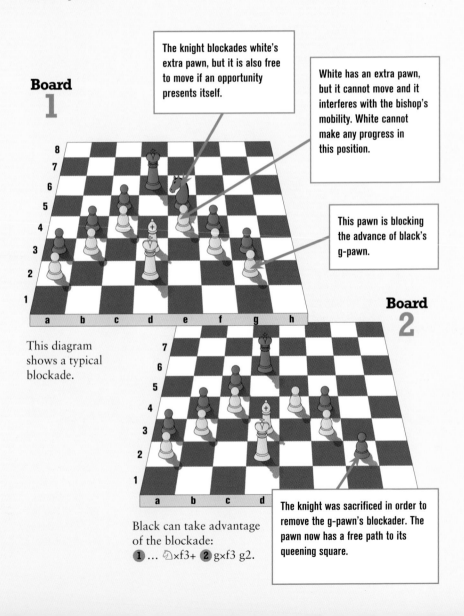

Board 1

The knight blockades white's extra pawn, but it is also free to move if an opportunity presents itself.

White has an extra pawn, but it cannot move and it interferes with the bishop's mobility. White cannot make any progress in this position.

This pawn is blocking the advance of black's g-pawn.

This diagram shows a typical blockade.

Board 2

Black can take advantage of the blockade:

1 … ♘xf3+ **2** gxf3 g2.

The knight was sacrificed in order to remove the g-pawn's blockader. The pawn now has a free path to its queening square.

The Bad Bishop

The Bad Bishop If your pawns are on the same color squares as your bishop, they may restrict its mobility. Since a piece's power is directly related to its mobility, an immobile bishop is worth less than a mobile one, and is termed a *bad bishop*.

The queen is attacking the pawn on a2 in order to provoke it to move. Alekhine is driving it from a light-colored square to a dark one.

The pawn cannot be defended and must advance.
1 b3 fails to
1 ... a×b3
2 a×b3 ♕×b3.

Board 1

Example 1: This position is from the game Tylor–Alekhine, Hastings 1936.

Board 2

The pawn is attacked by both the bishop on d4 and the queen on c2 and must fall.

This bishop is merely a passive defender.

White is forced to move the a-pawn to a black square, permanently blocking the bishop:
1 a3 b3 **2** e4 ♕c4 **3** ♕e1 ♕c2
4 f4 ♗c5+ **5** ♔h1 ♗d4.

The Bad Bishop continued

Example 2: If you must place your pawns on the same color as your bishop, try to make certain that the bishop is in front of the pawns and not behind them.

The following configuration may be quite acceptable:

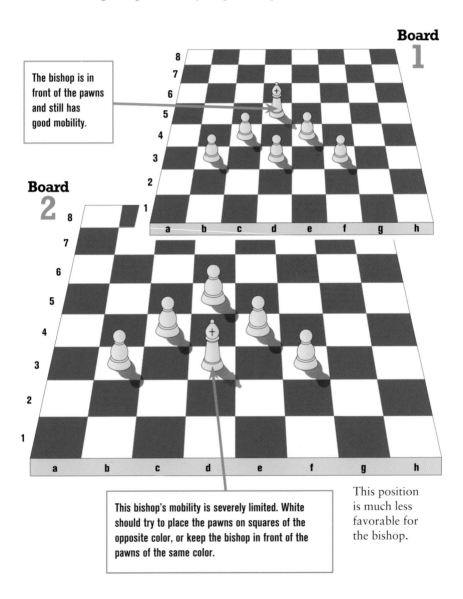

The bishop is in front of the pawns and still has good mobility.

Board 1

Board 2

This bishop's mobility is severely limited. White should try to place the pawns on squares of the opposite color, or keep the bishop in front of the pawns of the same color.

This position is much less favorable for the bishop.

Levers
Levers are pawn moves which help to pry open a position. Since pawns cannot attack the square in front of them, they need assistance in combating hostile forces positioned there.

Levers are useful tools whenever a position is blocked by pawns.

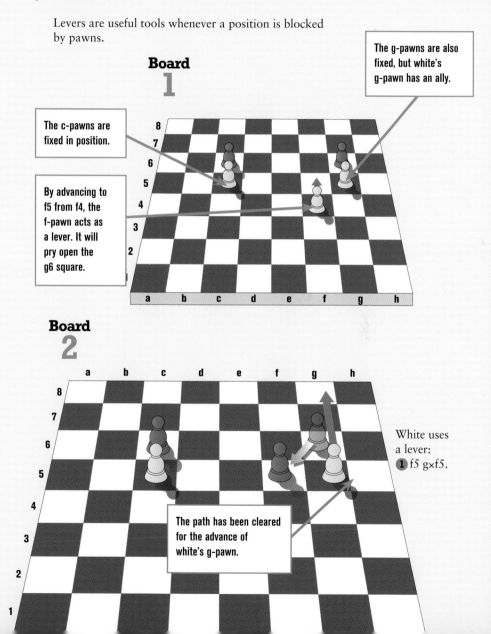

Board 1

The g-pawns are also fixed, but white's g-pawn has an ally.

The c-pawns are fixed in position.

By advancing to f5 from f4, the f-pawn acts as a lever. It will pry open the g6 square.

Board 2

White uses a lever:
1 f5 g×f5.

The path has been cleared for the advance of white's g-pawn.

Key Squares Some squares assume more importance than others during the course of the game. The struggle for control over such squares often dictates subsequent play. When key squares can be controlled by one player's pawns and not the others, they are called *outposts*. Knights in particular relish outposts and gain considerable strength when posted on one.

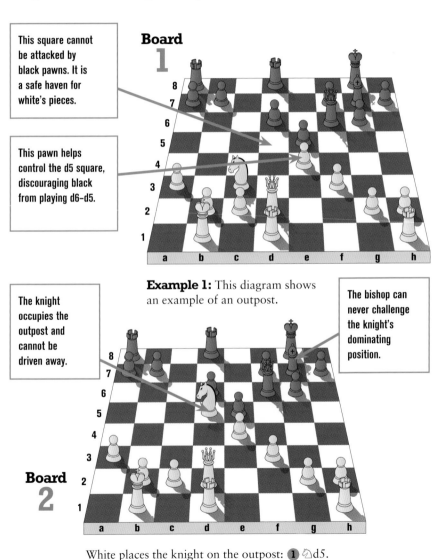

Board 1

This square cannot be attacked by black pawns. It is a safe haven for white's pieces.

This pawn helps control the d5 square, discouraging black from playing d6–d5.

Example 1: This diagram shows an example of an outpost.

The knight occupies the outpost and cannot be driven away.

The bishop can never challenge the knight's dominating position.

Board 2

White places the knight on the outpost: **1** ♘d5.

Key Squares continued

Example 2: Undefended squares in your position are like having a hole in one's protective armor. In fact, these squares are often referred to as *holes*. If the pieces and pawns are especially poorly coordinated, they may result in what is called a *weak color complex*. The following position occurred in the game Bernstein–Mieses, Coburg 1904.

Most of black's pawns have been fixed on light squares. They cannot protect against an invasion along the dark ones.

The bishop cannot defend the weak dark squares.

White has placed his pieces on dark squares, where they are nearly immune from capture.

Board 1

Black will not be able to defend both pawns.

Board 2

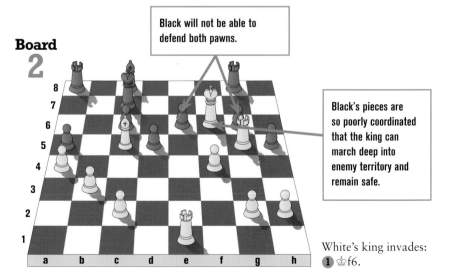

Black's pieces are so poorly coordinated that the king can march deep into enemy territory and remain safe.

White's king invades:
1 ♔f6.

Mastery Challenges VII

☞ For answers, see pp.158 and 159

"Even a poor plan is better than no plan at all."

Mikhail Chigorin (Russian, 1850–1908)

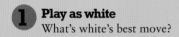

Play as white
What's white's best move?

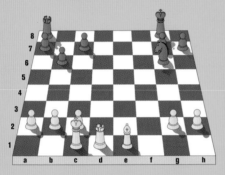

2 Best move
What's white's best move in this scenario?

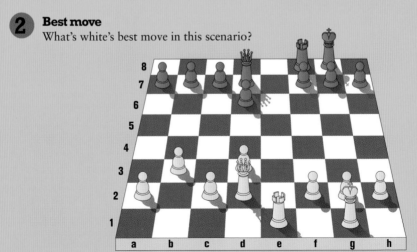

3 **Play it safe**
Make a safety-first move for black.

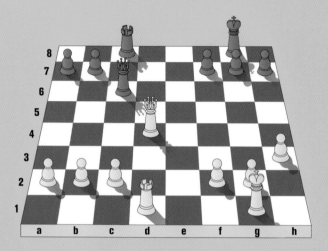

4 **Advise white**
Should white capture
the bishop?

5 **Consider both sides**
Who's in a better situation—black
or white?

6 **Help the knight**
Get white's knight to a key square.

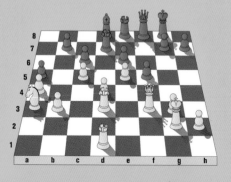

7 **Get some leverage**
Find a lever that frees black's rooks.

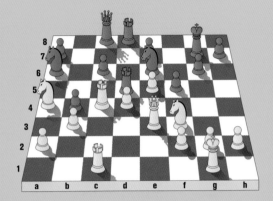

8 **Look ahead! Pawn majority**
Who has a kingside pawn majority?

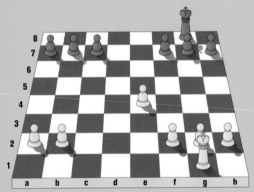

ANSWERS

1 **1. Rd7!.** You should make this move almost automatically. Your rook stands on an open file and has an opportunity to occupy your opponent's second rank—so, as a general principle, grab it! After 1. Rd7, black can try to hang onto his c–pawn with **1. … Rc8.** But then white has **2. Bc3,** double-attacking and winning black's g7–pawn. Good things tend to happen when you occupy the 7th rank!

2   **1. Qe2!**. White seizes the opportunity to double on the file, creating a battery with his rook and queen. There is no forced win, but the position is then a lot easier for white to play because black can't easily oppose white on the e–file.

3   **1. ... h6 or 1. ... g6** gives black *Luft*, an escape square from a potential backrank mate. On the other hand, greedy pawn-grabbing with 1. ... Qxc2?? would immediately be punished by 2. Qd8+! Rxd8 3. Rxd8#.

4   No! White should keep his knight on its dominating outpost. The true relative values of the knight and bishop depend on the game position. Here black's bishop is hemmed in by friendly pawns. A good move for white is 1. Rf7!—hitting the 7th rank with the threat of 2. Rxd7.

5   **White is winning,** no matter whose move it is. Notice that the short-ranged knight is trapped out of action on the far edge of the board by the long-range bishop, which corrals the knight while at the same time controlling the a2–g8 diagonal. Suppose it's black's move: 1. ... Kh8 2. Kg6—and white gobbles up black's pawns and will promote his own. If it's white's move, he uses an advanced king-moving technique called *triangulation* to pass the move back to black: 1. Ke6 Kg6 2. Ke5 Kg7 3. Kf5.

6   White's knight on the rim can relocate to the dominating outpost on d6 in two moves: **1. Nc4 Bc7 2. Nd6.** It's true that black could then trade his bishop for the knight, but after 2. ... Bxd6, 3. cxd6 gives white a strong protected passed pawn and a winning position. The diagram is from Botvinnik–Flohr, 1936. Twelve years later, Botvinnik was to become World Champion.

7   **1. ... c5** is the lever that will open the d–file (Furman–Ribli, 1975).

8   White has more pawns on the kingside than black does. So we say **white has a kingside majority**. With more pawns on the queenside, **black has a queenside majority**.

Section 8: PAWNS

The course of a game of chess is strongly influenced by the pawns. The general structure of the white and black pawns determines the strategy of the game, while particular strengths and weaknesses of individual pawns can be exploited for tactical or strategic advantage.

Pawn Formations

Correct conduct of the game is often determined by the arrangement of pawns. Certain pawn formations have become so well known that chess players have given them names. The best strategies for both sides facing these have been worked out over time. There is plenty of individual variation from game to game, but general strategic ideas remain constant.

The Fianchetto Fianchetto (pronounced fyan-ket-to) is an Italian word which means "on the flank." In chess terms, the word applies to a particular pawn and bishop formation. The formation has strengths and weaknesses, but has become a mainstay in modern chess play.

This is *not* a fianchettoed bishop.

This is a fianchetto formation.

The fianchetto positions the bishop on one of the longest diagonals. In this case it is the h1–a8 diagonal.

Example 1: This diagram shows a fianchettoed bishop.

Example 2: The fianchetto formation can be a tough nut to crack. It is usually safe to castle behind it, as in Board 1.

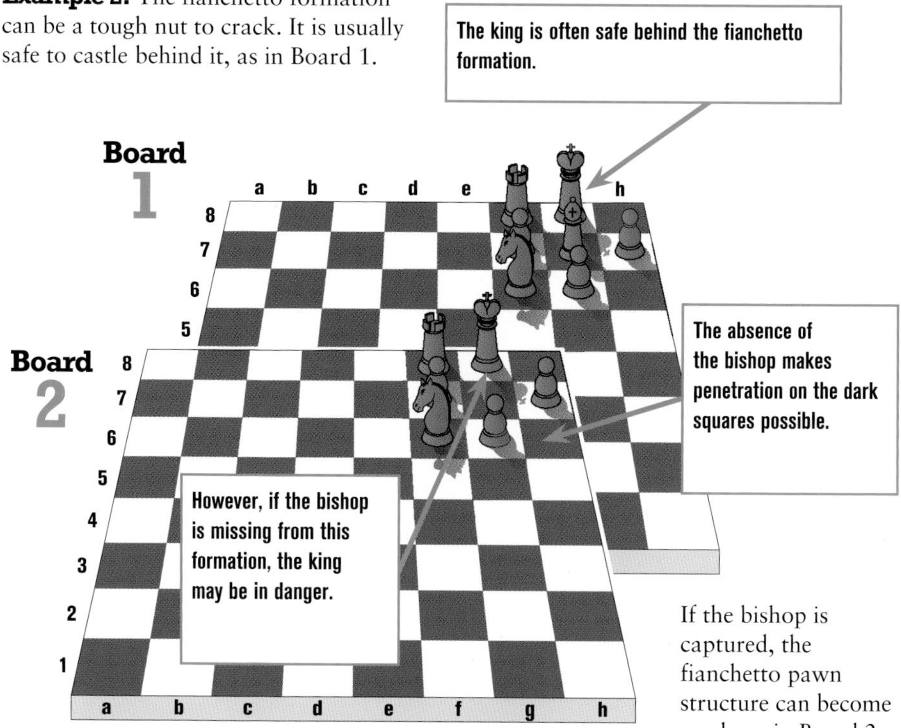
The king is often safe behind the fianchetto formation.
Board 1
a b c d e h
8 7 6 5
Board 2
8 7 6 5 4 3 2 1
a b c d e f g h
The absence of the bishop makes penetration on the dark squares possible.
However, if the bishop is missing from this formation, the king may be in danger.

If the bishop is captured, the fianchetto pawn structure can become weak, as in Board 2.

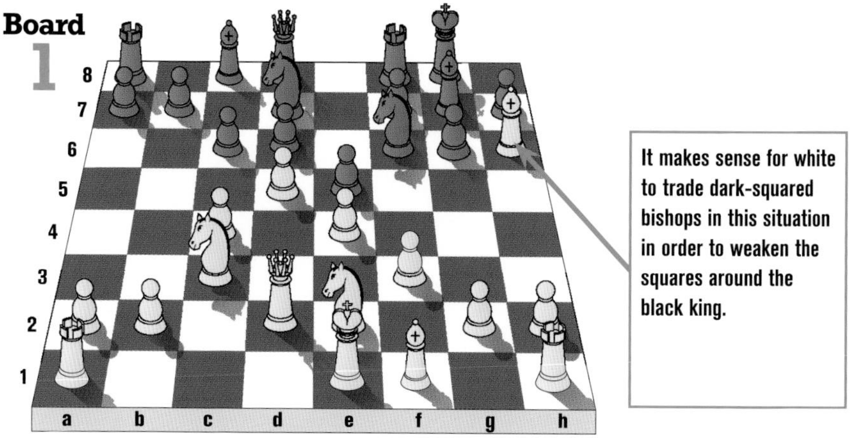
Board 1
8 7 6 5 4 3 2 1
a b c d e f g h
It makes sense for white to trade dark-squared bishops in this situation in order to weaken the squares around the black king.

Example 3: This position shows a typical method of exchanging off the fianchettoed bishop.

Board 2

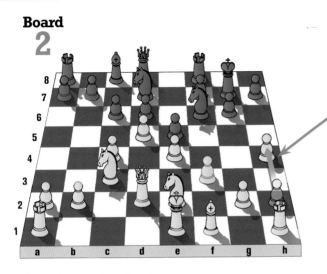

If the fianchettoed bishop is missing, try to open additional lines against the enemy king.

This is the situation after the moves:
1 ♗×g7 ♚×g7 **2** h4.

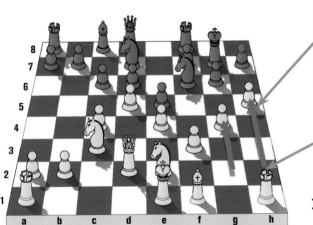

Black should try to prevent the pawn's advance, perhaps by playing h7–h5 earlier.

White will try to pry open the g- and h-files by exchanging pawns.

Board 3

Now white can attack the weakened king with the g- and h-pawns. ☞ See pp.79, 82, 84, and 88 for more examples of fianchettoed bishops.

King's Indian Formation

The King's Indian relies on an early kingside fianchetto by black. It has become one of the most popular and reliable defenses to ① d4.

Board 1

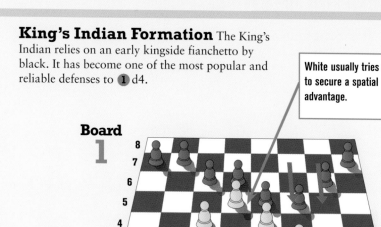

White usually tries to secure a spatial advantage.

Generally, black will try to attack on the kingside by advancing pawns and opening lines.

Board 2

White will try to eliminate the black d-pawn, allowing the pawn on d5 to advance.

Black will try to open and exploit the g-file.

This is how the pawn structure might develop.
☞ See p.82 for more examples of typical King's Indian pawn structures.

Dragon Formation Naming conventions in chess are at times eccentric. For example, the Dragon was named after a constellation of stars. It too relies on a kingside fianchetto.

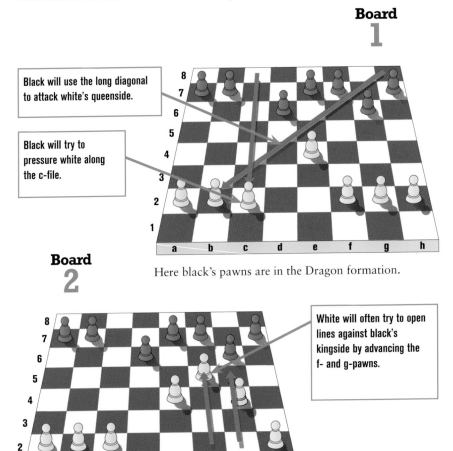

Board 1

Black will use the long diagonal to attack white's queenside.

Black will try to pressure white along the c-file.

Here black's pawns are in the Dragon formation.

Board 2

White will often try to open lines against black's kingside by advancing the f- and g-pawns.

This diagram shows one way for white to attack the Dragon formation. ☛ See p.69 for more about the Sicilian Dragon.

Advanced French

Black will try to eliminate white's d-pawn, which will in turn weaken white's e-pawn.

White's e-pawn cramps black's position. Black will try to undermine and destroy it.

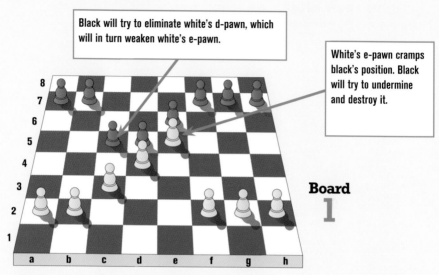

Board 1

This formation is extremely common in the French Defense.

Board 2

White has successfully maintained the e-pawn and will have a spatial advantage.

Now this pawn may only be attacked by pieces. It should be relatively easy to defend it.

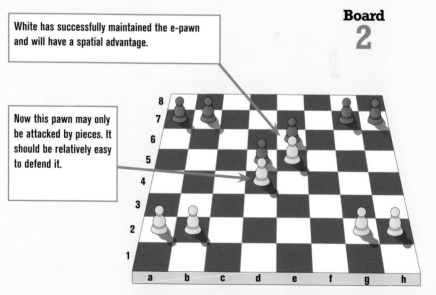

If white's plan is successful, this pawn structure may arise.

Closed English White tries to control the d5
square by a combination of a kingside fianchetto and the
c-pawn. If black does not contest the d5 square the
position in the center may remain closed for some time.

Black can counter by
trying to control and
occupy d4 in return.

Combined with the
kingside fianchetto,
white tries to control
d5 with the c-pawn.

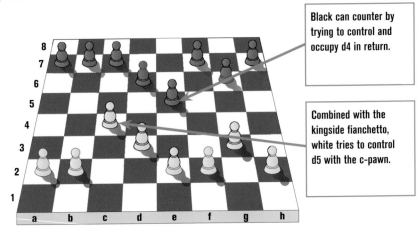

Board Here is a typical Closed English structure.

1

Black often plays f5–f4 in order
to attack on the kingside.

Board

2

White often expands on
the queenside, which
makes the kingside
fianchetto even more
effective.

As the game progresses, the pawn structure might
develop like this.

Caro–Kann and Slav Formations

In these formations white has a pawn on d4, and black tries to prevent its further advance by controlling the d5 square.

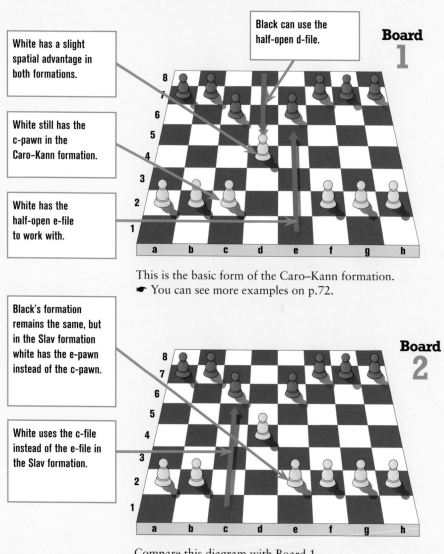

Black can use the half-open d-file.

Board 1

White has a slight spatial advantage in both formations.

White still has the c-pawn in the Caro-Kann formation.

White has the half-open e-file to work with.

This is the basic form of the Caro–Kann formation.

☞ You can see more examples on p.72.

Black's formation remains the same, but in the Slav formation white has the e-pawn instead of the c-pawn.

Board 2

White uses the c-file instead of the e-file in the Slav formation.

Compare this diagram with Board 1.

☞ See p.78 for more on the Slav formation.

The Scheveningen The Scheveningen is one of the more flexible pawn formations and is seen quite often in the games of the world's best players. Black has an extra center pawn and active counterplay on the queenside, while white retains a special advantage and attacking chances in the center and on the kingside.

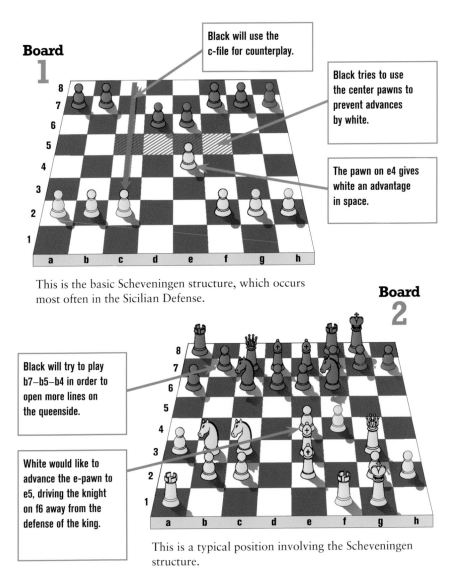

Board 1

Black will use the c-file for counterplay.

Black tries to use the center pawns to prevent advances by white.

The pawn on e4 gives white an advantage in space.

This is the basic Scheveningen structure, which occurs most often in the Sicilian Defense.

Board 2

Black will try to play b7–b5–b4 in order to open more lines on the queenside.

White would like to advance the e-pawn to e5, driving the knight on f6 away from the defense of the king.

This is a typical position involving the Scheveningen structure.

The Isolated Queen's Pawn Positions with an isolated queen's pawn (IQP) arise from many different openings, such as the Queen's Gambit and the French Defense. It is often unclear whether the isolated pawn represents a strength or a weakness. If one must passively defend the pawn, it can be a liability. However, it may also serve as a springboard to attack.

White will try to use the spatial advantage conferred by the d-pawn to launch an attack.

The d5 square is of primary importance. If black can prevent the d-pawn's advance, it may turn into a liability for white.

Example 1: This is the fundamental IQP structure.

If black can establish a blockade on d5, white often drifts into passivity. The knight cannot be driven away by white's pawns, so it can be difficult for white to break the blockade.

The pawn tends to grow weaker as more pieces are exchanged.

Control of the c-file is an important consideration in this type of formation.

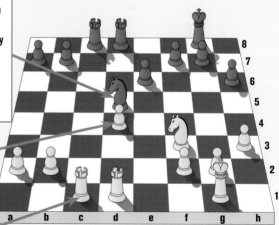

Example 2: This diagram highlights some of the themes in IQP positions. ☛ More examples can be found on p.182.

The Isolated Queen's Pawn continued

Example 3: The famous game Petrosian–Balashov, USSR 1974, featured a successful advance of the isolated queen's pawn, which caused black's position to fall apart.

Board 1

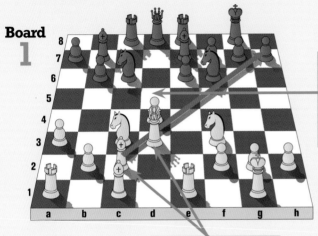

Black probably thought that the d5 square was under his control. His queen, knight on f6, and pawn on e6 all attack it.

This was the position reached after the opening.

This battery is a powerful attacking formation.

Petrosian launched an attack by playing:
1 d5 e×d5 **2** ♗g5 ♘e4 **3** ♘×e4 d×e4
4 ♕×e4 g6 **5** ♕h4 ♕c7 **6** ♗b3.

Board 2

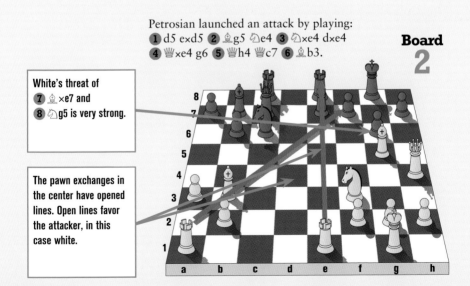

White's threat of
7 ♗×e7 and
8 ♘g5 is very strong.

The pawn exchanges in the center have opened lines. Open lines favor the attacker, in this case white.

Queen's Gambit Declined

Black often chooses to maintain a pawn on d5 in the Queen's Gambit Declined. The pawn is supported by either the c-pawn or e-pawn, or in many cases both. The typical pawn formation is depicted below.

This pawn represents the key to black's strategy. It allows black to maintain a strong presence in the center, specifically by controlling the light squares d5 and e4.

Black would like to be able to control this square.

Board

1

Black has the option of recapturing with the e-pawn or the c-pawn. Black might be able to recapture with a piece, but this would lead to a weakened center.

When white chooses to capture c×d5, it is called the *Exchange Variation* of the Queen's Gambit Declined.

One option for white is to capture on d5.

Board

2

Queen's Gambit Declined continued

Recapturing with the c-pawn leads to a symmetrical position. Usually, white maintains a slight advantage in symmetrical positions by virtue of moving first.

Both sides will try to control the only open file. If neither side is able to control the file, a series of exchanges may take place. Such exchanges tend to produce colorless positions often ending in draws.

This is the pawn structure after recapturing with the c-pawn.

Board 3

This diagonal is open, which increases the scope of black's light square bishop.

Blacks can use the e-file to pressurize white's position with the rooks and queen.

Board 4

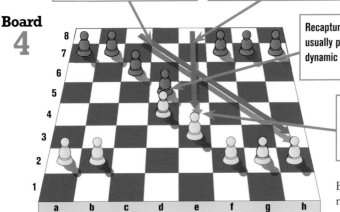

Recapturing with the e-pawn usually produces a more dynamic game.

The black knights would love to occupy this square.

Black can also recapture with the e-pawn. ☛ See p.76 for another example.

Minority Attack Although in the preceding variation of the Queen's Gambit Declined the black queenside pawns outnumber white's, they are vulnerable to a special sort of assault called the *minority attack*. White will advance the a- and b-pawns in order to force black on the defensive.

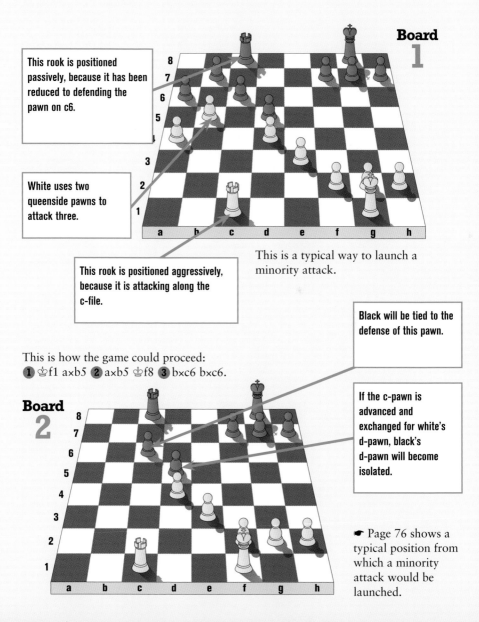

Board 1

This rook is positioned passively, because it has been reduced to defending the pawn on c6.

White uses two queenside pawns to attack three.

This rook is positioned aggressively, because it is attacking along the c-file.

This is a typical way to launch a minority attack.

Black will be tied to the defense of this pawn.

This is how the game could proceed:
1 ♔f1 a×b5 **2** a×b5 ♔f8 **3** b×c6 b×c6.

If the c-pawn is advanced and exchanged for white's d-pawn, black's d-pawn will become isolated.

Board 2

☞ Page 76 shows a typical position from which a minority attack would be launched.

Nimzo–Botvinnik Formation

This formation is characterized by pawns on c4 and e4, as well as a kingside fianchetto. White piles up pressure on the light squares in the center and prepares for expansion on either wing.

Board 1

These pawns help secure a strong foothold in the center. White will be able to launch operations on either wing without fear of reprisal in the center.

The main drawback of this system is the lack of control over the d4 square. Black should try to exploit this.

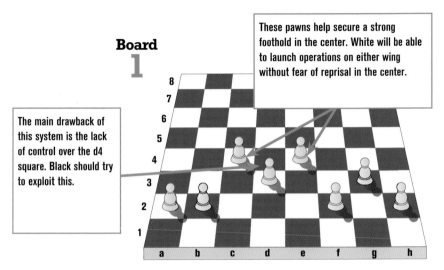

This is the basic Nimzo–Botvinnik formation.

Board 2

This knight has made a long trip (f6–e8–c7) in order to go to e6. From there it will exert even more control over d4.

Black can counter this formation by controlling and occupying d4.

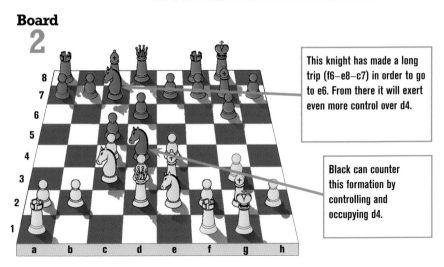

This position is typical of the Nimzo–Botvinnik pawn structure.

The Bayonet Attack The *bayonet attack* is the term given to a single pawn's advance against the enemy king. The pawn charges into the teeth of the enemy defenses. It may become lost, but its advance often disorganizes the opponent's defenders and paves the way for the troops that follow. This position occurred in the game Alekhine–Weenink, Prague 1931.

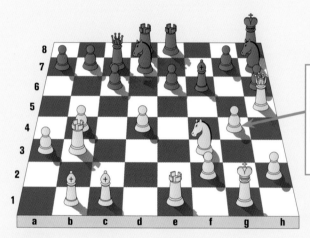

White has just played g2-g4. This pawn is now threatening to disrupt black's kingside defenses by advancing to g5.

Board
1

White launches a bayonet attack.

The game continued:
1 ... ♛d6 **2** ♝g6 ♜f8 **3** g5.

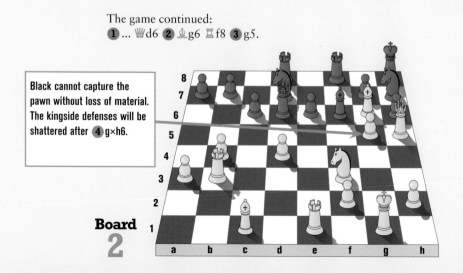

Black cannot capture the pawn without loss of material. The kingside defenses will be shattered after **4** g×h6.

Board
2

Strengths and Weaknesses

As with everything else in chess, weaknesses are relative. An isolated pawn on the 7th rank poised to become a queen can hardly be called a weakness. However, assuming all things to be equal, weaknesses in pawn structure can have a telling effect upon a game's outcome. These weaknesses become ever more influential as the game progresses toward its ending.

Pawn Chains When two or more pawns are connected diagonally, they are called a *chain*. A pawn chain can be very powerful, because it can restrict the mobility of enemy pieces and pawns. However, the base of the chain is its weakest link.

Capturing the white d-pawn would transfer the base to d4, but it would not destroy the chain.

This is the base of the pawn chain f7, e6, and d5.

This is the base of the pawn chain c3, d4, and e5.

Once its base is destroyed the former head of the chain becomes easier to attack.

By attacking the pawn chain at its base, black is able to destroy it. If **3** c×b4 c×d4 then the chain is destroyed.

This diagram shows two pawn chains.

Black attacks the base of the white pawn chain: **1** ... b4!

☛ Pawn chains like this are typical of the French Defense (p.71).

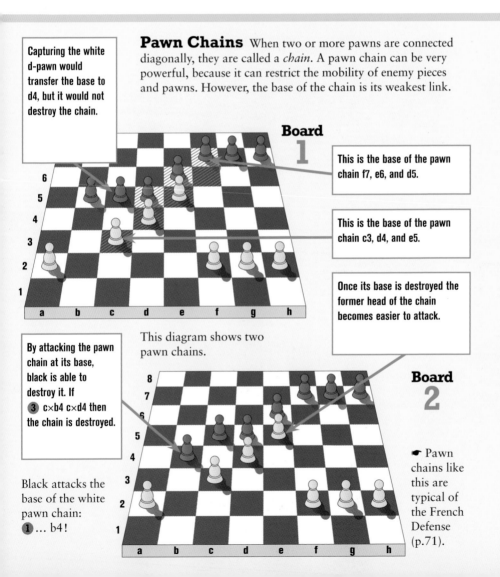

Board 1

Board 2

Pawn Islands

When groups of pawns are separated from one another they are called *pawn islands*. "Less is more" in this case, where the side with fewer islands is usually stronger.

> **The b- and c-pawns constitute one island.**

> **The f- and e-pawns are another.**

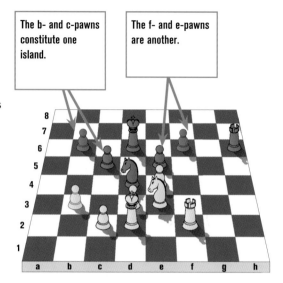

Board 1

This diagram illustrates the concept.

> **The knight attacks one pawn in each island, and one of them must fall.**

> **White's pawns are all in one island and are easier to protect.**

Board 2

White can exploit the black pawn islands by playing: ❶ ♘d5.

Pawn Majorities Healthy pawn majorities constitute a potential advantage because they may be used to create a passed pawn. Simply the threat of creating a passed pawn may be sufficient to force the opposition into passivity.

> Black has a crippled pawn majority on the queenside—the doubled pawns make it hard to create a passed pawn.

> White has a four versus three pawn majority on the kingside.

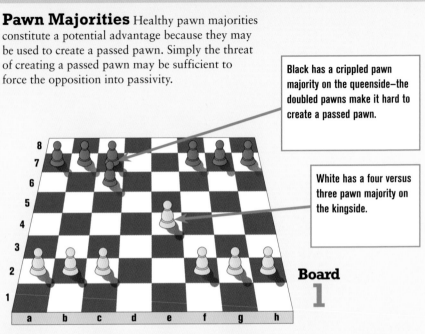

Board 1

☛ This pawn structure often occurs in the Berlin Defense of the Ruy Lopez (p.58).

Board 2

> If black were to somehow succeed in exchanging c-pawns in Board 1, the result would be a three versus two pawn majority on the queenside. A three versus two pawn majority is slightly preferable to four versus three because a passed pawn may be generated more quickly.

White's advantage is on the kingside, while black's is on the queenside.

Passed Pawns A passed pawn is a pawn with no enemy counterpart in its path, either on the same file or on adjoining files. The advance of such pawns can only be prevented by enemy pieces. Pieces tied down by a pawn are rarely at their best.

Board 1

The king will be forced to the a-file in order to stop the pawn. This will free the white king to gobble up black's kingside pawns.

This pawn is an outside passed pawn. Although material is equal, this pawn is a winning advantage because it decoys the white king.

In this position, material is equal but white has a passed pawn.

Board 2

Play could continue:
1 a5 ♚b5 **2** ♚d5 ♚xa5 **3** ♚e6 f5 **4** gxf5 gxf5
5 ♚xf5 ♚b6 **6** ♚g6 ♚c7 **7** ♚xh6 ♚d7 **8** h5 ♚e7 **9** ♚g7.

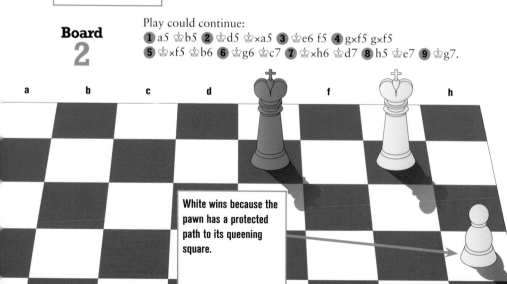

White wins because the pawn has a protected path to its queening square.

Rook Pawns

Pawns on the a- or h-files are also called *rook pawns*. Passed rook pawns can be especially useful for distracting enemy pieces. However, they do have one serious drawback. They cannot, by themselves or with the aid of a king, drive an enemy king away from their queening squares.

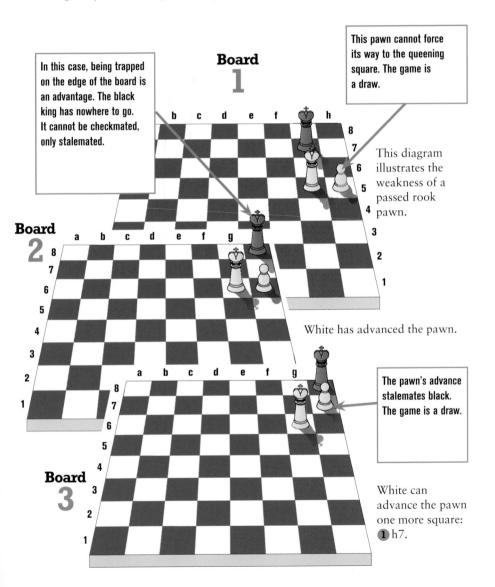

This pawn cannot force its way to the queening square. The game is a draw.

Board 1

In this case, being trapped on the edge of the board is an advantage. The black king has nowhere to go. It cannot be checkmated, only stalemated.

This diagram illustrates the weakness of a passed rook pawn.

Board 2

White has advanced the pawn.

Board 3

The pawn's advance stalemates black. The game is a draw.

White can advance the pawn one more square: **1** h7.

Protected Passed Pawns

Protected Passed Pawns A passed pawn that is defended by another pawn is called a *protected passed pawn*. The strength of the forward pawn is still determined by its mobility, but it is at least relatively immune to capture.

This pawn is a protected passed pawn. The white king cannot capture it. However, if it advances it will be lost.

Board 1

This curious position arose in the game Siff–Eade, USA 1984.

The king cannot capture the b-pawn, because black would then queen the c-pawn. It is a standoff.

Whichever of these two pawns advances will turn into a protected passed pawn. The black king cannot capture the pawns, but it can blockade their further advance. This is also a standoff and the game was agreed drawn.

Black's d-pawn is a protected passed pawn.

White has immobilized the protected passed pawn, sapping it of its power.

Board 2

Protected passed pawns are not always significant, as this position shows.

Isolated Pawns A pawn is considered isolated when there are no pawns of the same color on adjoining files. If isolated pawns come under attack, they may constitute a weakness, because they have no neighboring pawn to assist in their defense. The square immediately in front of an isolated pawn cannot be attacked by other pawns and may become a nice perch for an enemy piece.

This rook is preventing the advance of the pawn. This is called a *blockade*.

This pawn is isolated. It has come under attack by the black pieces.

White's pieces have been reduced to defending the b-pawn.

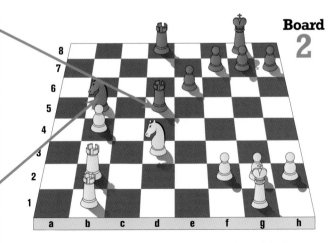

Board 1

In this position, white has a passed pawn, but it is also isolated.

Once a blockade is established, the other pieces are free to wreak as much havoc as possible.

The knight is an ideal blockader, because it loses none of its power and cannot be easily driven away.

Board 2

The passive nature of white's position allows black to reorganize and apply pressure elsewhere.

An advanced isolated pawn might be a horse of a different color. If it is well supported it can tie down the enemy pieces in a desperate bid to halt its advance.

The rook is preventing the advance of the b-pawn, but it cannot move away.

The rooks are supporting the b-pawn. They guard against its capture and will allow it to queen if the rook on b8 can be deflected away.

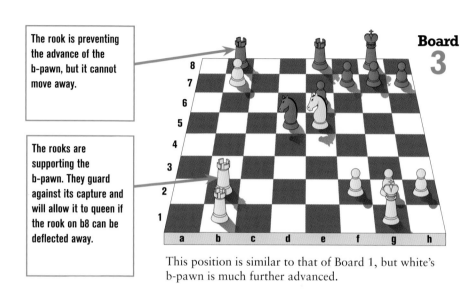

Board 3

This position is similar to that of Board 1, but white's b-pawn is much further advanced.

White wins by playing: **1** ♘c6.

Simply by attacking the blockader, white wins material.

If black had used the knight to blockade the b-pawn instead of the rook, there would be no loss of material.

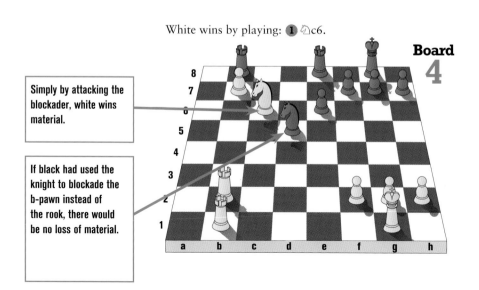

Board 4

Backward Pawns A backward pawn is not technically isolated, but it has been left behind by its peers. Its advance cannot be supported by neighboring pawns. Although no enemy pawn stands directly in its path, its advance is constrained by one on an adjoining file. Backward pawns were considered serious weaknesses by the classical school, but that evaluation has changed. In particular, a well-timed advance of the backward pawn can cause a fair amount of havoc.

Consider this variation of the French Defense:

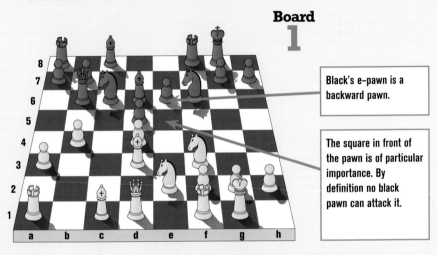

Board 1

Black's e-pawn is a backward pawn.

The square in front of the pawn is of particular importance. By definition no black pawn can attack it.

This position arises from a game beginning: **1** e4 e6 **2** d4 d5 **3** ♘d2 ♘f6 **4** e5 ♘fd7 **5** ♗d3 c5 **6** c3 ♘c6 **7** ♘e2 ♕b6 **8** ♘f3 cxd4 **9** cxd4 f6 **10** exf6 ♘xf6 **11** 0–0 ♗d6 **12** a3 0–0 **13** b4.

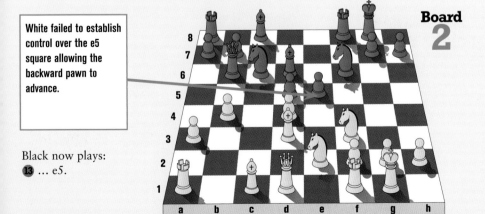

Board 2

White failed to establish control over the e5 square allowing the backward pawn to advance.

Black now plays:
13 ... e5.

Hanging Pawns The term refers to a pawn island consisting of two united pawns on half-open files. One of the pawns must be on one of the four central files. Hanging pawns occur most commonly on the c- and d-files. They may be strong if they are mobile and help to control key central squares. However, if one of the pawns advances, the trailing pawn may become backward and weak.

The squares attacked by these pawns usually play a pivotal role in determining whether the hanging pawns are strong or weak.

White's c– and d–pawns constitute hanging pawns.

Example 1: This is a typical hanging pawn structure.

A wing pawn is frequently used to attack hanging pawns. An exchange will leave a lone isolated pawn. If the attacked pawn advances instead, both pawns may get blockaded.

If one of the pawns is forced to advance, the trailing pawn may become backward. White's d-pawn has been blockaded, forcing white to use pieces in order to defend it.

Example 2: This position shows what can happen if one of the hanging pawns advances.

Hanging Pawns continued

Example 3: Hanging pawns may be advanced voluntarily if the right opportunity presents itself. This is especially true if the pawns are supporting an attack against the enemy king.

White has just played d4–d5 opening the a1–h8 diagonal for white's bishop on c3.

The bishop springs to life after the pawn advances.

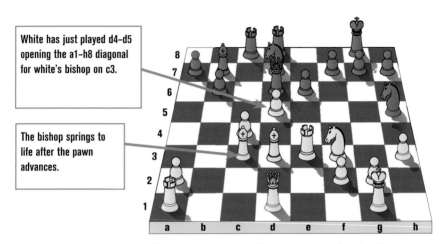

This position occurred in the game Gligoric–Keres, Yugoslavia 1958.

The hanging pawns can also be effective when supporting a knight on e5, as in this position from the game Botvinnik–Chekhover, Russia 1935.

The hanging pawns control the center, allowing white to advance the f-pawn in safety. The further advance f4–f5 threatens to disrupt black's defenses.

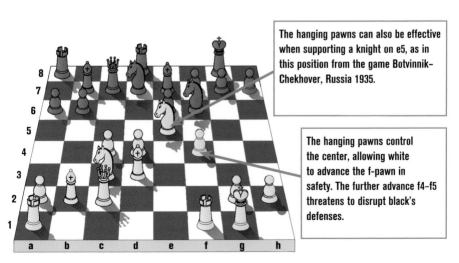

Example 4: Here is another example of the usefulness of hanging pawns.

Doubled Pawns

Doubled Pawns Two pawns of the same color on the same file are called *doubled pawns*. Doubled pawns suffer a slight loss of mobility and lose the ability to protect one another. (Even worse are tripled pawns.) On the other hand, the side with doubled pawns has an extra file to work with, and sometimes the doubled pawns can control key squares in ways healthy ones could not.

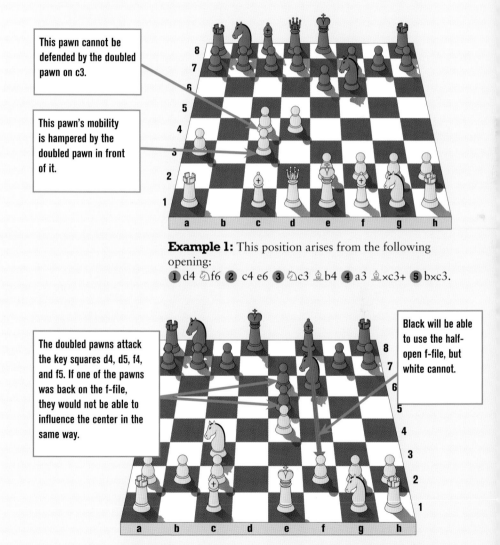

This pawn cannot be defended by the doubled pawn on c3.

This pawn's mobility is hampered by the doubled pawn in front of it.

Example 1: This position arises from the following opening:
1 d4 ♘f6 **2** c4 e6 **3** ♘c3 ♗b4 **4** a3 ♗xc3+ **5** bxc3.

The doubled pawns attack the key squares d4, d5, f4, and f5. If one of the pawns was back on the f-file, they would not be able to influence the center in the same way.

Black will be able to use the half-open f-file, but white cannot.

Example 2: In this case, the doubled black pawns are effective. Their influence on the center compensates for any weakness.

Mastery Challenges VIII

☛ For answers, see p.191

"Pawns are the soul of chess."

Francois-Andre Philidor (1726–1795)

1 **Opening traps**
No matter how good the opening formation, chess players have to be alert. Early mistakes can lead to sudden disasters. Answer the question below each of the boards.

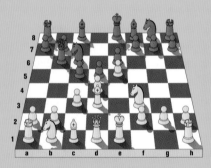

A. Advanced French
Black's move: Should black win a pawn on d4?

B. English opening
White's move: Should white capture the bishop on b4?

2   Caro-Kann variations

After the moves 1. e4 c6 2. d4 d5 3. Nc3 dxe4 4. Nxe4, we have the position below in the Caro-Kann. Two of black's popular responses are 4. … Nf6 and 4. … Nd7:

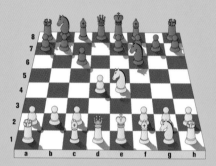

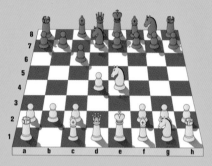

A. After 4. … Nf6, what's white's natural move?

B. After 4. … Nd7, what do you think black intends next?

3   Weak pawns

In the board right, identify:
A. Doubled pawns
B. Tripled pawns
C. Backward pawn
D. Isolated pawn

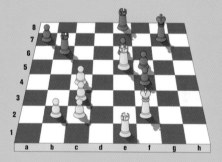

4   More pawn terminology

In the board right, identify:
A. Hanging pawns
B. Pawn chains
C. Remote passed pawn
D. Protected passed pawn

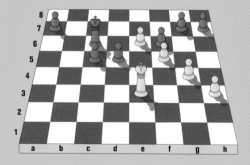

5 **Minority attack**
In the position shown to the right, what does white play to continue the minority attack?

6 **Match in formation**
Match each name of a pawn formation with a board.
King's Indian
Nimzo-Botvinnik
Isolated Queen's Pawn

Board A

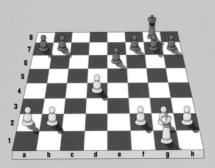

Board B

Board C

ANSWERS

1 **A. No.** The juicy pawn-win available to black on d4 is a famous trap. Let's see how it plays out if black falls all the way in: 1. ... cxd4 2. cxd4 Nxd4? 3. Nxd4 Qxd4??. Find a winning tactic for white in the position shown on the right. With 4. Bb5+!, white uncovers the attack on black's queen.

After 3. ... Qxd4??

B. No. 1. axb4??? (It's a *really* bad move!) overlooks the looming threat of mate-in-one. 1. ... Nf3#, when white can't capture the pawn because his e–pawn is pinned by the black queen. White weakened his fianchetto position by delaying Bg2 after he played g3.

2 **A. 5. Nxf6** doubles black's f–pawn on the spot.
B. Black intends 5. ... N(g)f6, when he can recapture on f6 with the other knight, avoiding a doubled pawn on the f–file.

3 **A.** The double pawns are on f5 and f4.
B. The tripled pawns are on c2, c3, and c4.
C. The backward pawn is on e6. (Its neighboring pawn has been pushed forward and so can't protect it.)
D. The isolated pawn is a7. (It has no friendly pawns adjacent to it.)

4 **A.** The hanging pawns are on c5 and d5.
B. The pawn chains are on the h3–e6 diagonal and on the g7–f6 diagonal.
C. The remote passed pawn is on a7.
D. The protected passed pawn is on e6.

5 **1. b5 continues the minority attack.** White wants to saddle black with an isolated pawn on an open file on the queenside.

6 A. Nimzo–Botvinnik
B. Isolated Queen's Pawn
C. King's Indian

Section 9: THE ENDGAME

A chess game is generally divided into three distinct phases: the opening, middlegame, and endgame. The endgame is characterized by the presence of relatively few pieces. The reduction in material creates a new world governed by different and sometimes paradoxical laws.

The Active King

You spend the better part of the game worrying about the king's safety, but in the endgame the king becomes emboldened because the danger of a checkmating attack is much reduced. Many endings are decided based on little more than which king is the more effective piece.

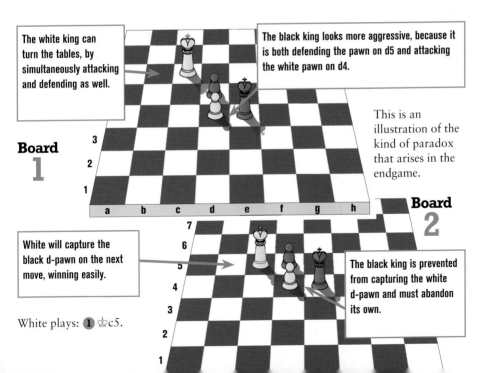

The white king can turn the tables, by simultaneously attacking and defending as well.

The black king looks more aggressive, because it is both defending the pawn on d5 and attacking the white pawn on d4.

This is an illustration of the kind of paradox that arises in the endgame.

Board 1

Board 2

White will capture the black d-pawn on the next move, winning easily.

The black king is prevented from capturing the white d-pawn and must abandon its own.

White plays: **1** ♔c5.

Zugzwang If compelled to make a move, when all moves are bad (as was the case for black on the preceding page), a player may be in zugzwang. Zugzwang is a German word that describes the situation where your position is alright as is, but will get worse if you have to move. You cannot pass in chess, although there are techniques, such as triangulation (☛ see p.201), that have that net effect. Zugzwang is not confined to endgames, but it rarely surfaces in any other phase of the game.

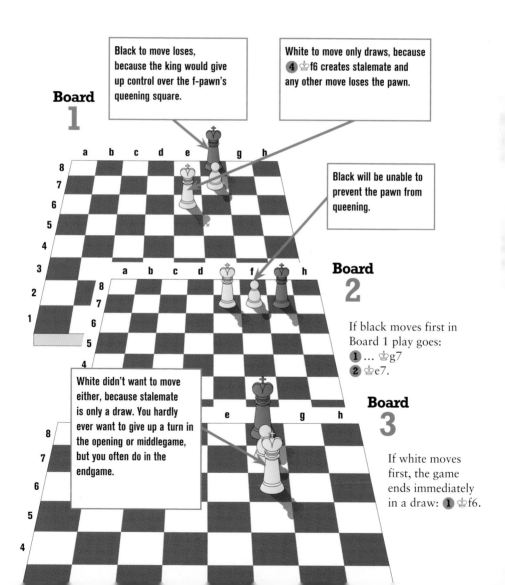

Black to move loses, because the king would give up control over the f-pawn's queening square.

White to move only draws, because **4** ♔f6 creates stalemate and any other move loses the pawn.

Board 1

Black will be unable to prevent the pawn from queening.

Board 2

If black moves first in Board 1 play goes:
1 ... ♔g7
2 ♔e7.

White didn't want to move either, because stalemate is only a draw. You hardly ever want to give up a turn in the opening or middlegame, but you often do in the endgame.

Board 3

If white moves first, the game ends immediately in a draw: **1** ♔f6.

Pawn Endings

These are sometimes called *king and pawn endings,* but the kings are a given. There's very little material to work with, but the beauty of pawns is that they can always make more material. Getting a pawn safely to the 8th rank and promoting it is the most common winning procedure. Despite their seeming simplicity, pawn endings can be surprisingly difficult to master. There are some techniques that must be thoroughly understood before you can play these endings well.

Rule Of The Square The simplest winning situation in a king and pawn versus king ending is when the pawn can simply queen without help from its own king. There is a quick way to tell whether this is possible. You mentally draw a line from the pawn to the queening square and then create a square in the direction of the enemy king. If the king is outside the square on your turn you can queen the pawn safely. However, if it is inside the square, or can move in it before your turn to play, it can stop the pawn.

The king is outside the square and cannot move into it on the next move. White can safely advance the pawn to its queening square and promote it.

The h8 square is the h-pawn's queening square.

Board 1

In this diagram, the black king is one square closer to the queening square (h8).

Now, the situation is different. You must know whose turn it is in order to know the outcome. If it is white's turn to move, the pawn can safely advance, because the black king is outside the square. If it is black's turn to move, black will move inside the square and capture the pawn.

Board 2

Kings First If you cannot simply queen the pawn by marching it directly to its queening square, you will be forced to use your king in order to help it advance. The kings will then do battle for control over the queening square. Both sides will try to get their king in front of the pawn.

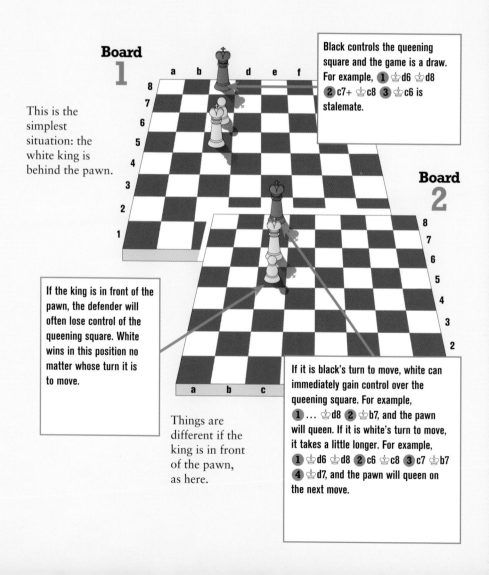

Board 1

This is the simplest situation: the white king is behind the pawn.

Black controls the queening square and the game is a draw. For example, **1** ♔d6 ♚d8 **2** c7+ ♚c8 **3** ♔c6 is stalemate.

Board 2

If the king is in front of the pawn, the defender will often lose control of the queening square. White wins in this position no matter whose turn it is to move.

Things are different if the king is in front of the pawn, as here.

If it is black's turn to move, white can immediately gain control over the queening square. For example, **1** ... ♚d8 **2** ♔b7, and the pawn will queen. If it is white's turn to move, it takes a little longer. For example, **1** ♔d6 ♚d8 **2** c6 ♚c8 **3** c7 ♚b7 **4** ♔d7, and the pawn will queen on the next move.

Opposition Opposition occurs when two kings face each other in a showdown where you don't want to be the one to move first. If we move the pieces back one rank from the example given on the previous page, we can illustrate the power of the opposition. Opposition is a form of zugzwang (☛ see p.193) specific to kings.

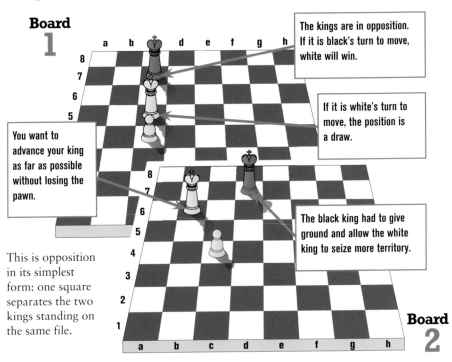

Board 1

The kings are in opposition. If it is black's turn to move, white will win.

If it is white's turn to move, the position is a draw.

You want to advance your king as far as possible without losing the pawn.

The black king had to give ground and allow the white king to seize more territory.

Board 2

This is opposition in its simplest form: one square separates the two kings standing on the same file.

Example 1: This is what happens if black moves first:
1 ... ♚d7 **2** ♔b6.

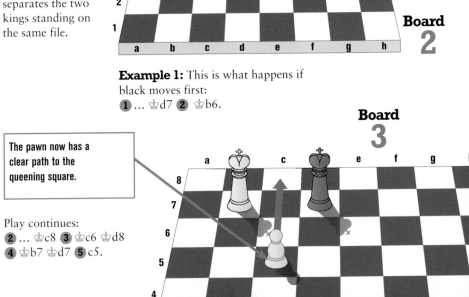

Board 3

The pawn now has a clear path to the queening square.

Play continues:
2 ... ♚c8 **3** ♔c6 ♚d8
4 ♔b7 ♚d7 **5** c5.

Opposition continued

Example 2: If it is white's turn to move, black has the opposition and can draw.

Black would have met
1 ♔d5 with
1 ... ♚d7, again
taking the opposition.

The white king cannot secure any more territory, so the pawn must advance. It isn't good enough to win.

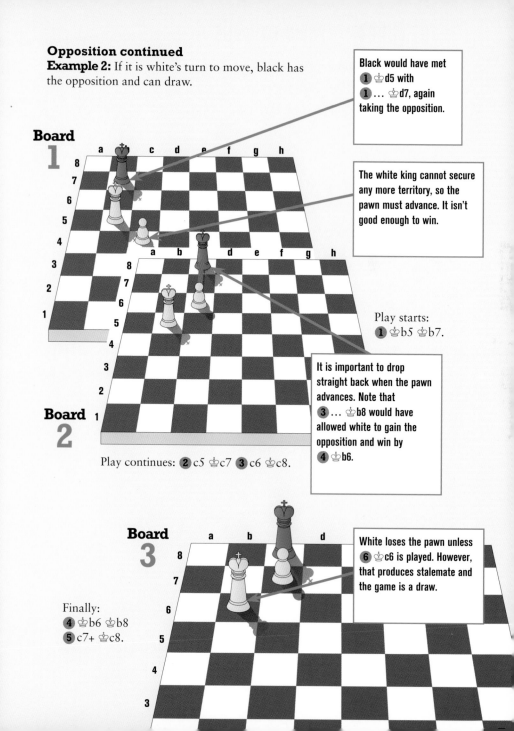

Board 1

Board 2

Play starts:
1 ♔b5 ♚b7.

It is important to drop straight back when the pawn advances. Note that
3 ... ♚b8 would have allowed white to gain the opposition and win by
4 ♔b6.

Play continues: 2 c5 ♚c7 3 c6 ♚c8.

Board 3

Finally:
4 ♔b6 ♚b8
5 c7+ ♚c8.

White loses the pawn unless
6 ♔c6 is played. However, that produces stalemate and the game is a draw.

Distant Opposition You have the distant opposition if it is your turn to play, and there are an even number of squares between the kings. This applies to files, ranks, and diagonals.

Board 1

There are six squares between the kings. Since six is an even number, whoever is to move will win.

In this position, whoever is on move has the distant opposition.

White started with distant opposition and turned it into direct opposition.

Play might continue:
1 ♔e2 ♚e7 **2** ♔e3 ♚e6
3 ♔e4.

Black must give ground and allow white to penetrate. White will win after **3** ... ♚f6
4 ♔f4 ♚g6
5 ♔e5.

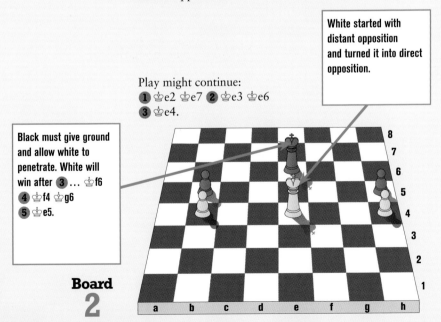

Board 2

Waiting Moves Waiting moves may occur at various points in a game, but they can be decisive in pawn endings. Having an extra pawn move might mean that you can use it to obtain the opposition.

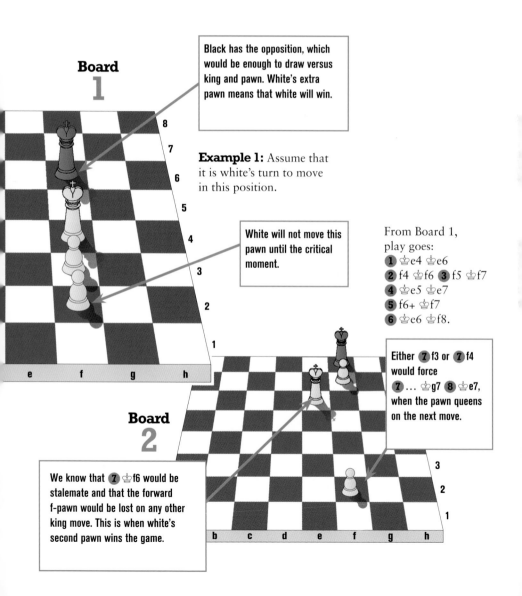

Black has the opposition, which would be enough to draw versus king and pawn. White's extra pawn means that white will win.

Board 1

Example 1: Assume that it is white's turn to move in this position.

White will not move this pawn until the critical moment.

From Board 1, play goes:
1 ♔e4 ♚e6
2 f4 ♚f6 **3** f5 ♚f7
4 ♔e5 ♚e7
5 f6+ ♚f7
6 ♔e6 ♚f8.

Either **7** f3 or **7** f4 would force
7 ... ♚g7 **8** ♔e7, when the pawn queens on the next move.

Board 2

We know that **7** ♔f6 would be stalemate and that the forward f-pawn would be lost on any other king move. This is when white's second pawn wins the game.

Example 2: Even without an extra pawn, an extra move can turn a draw into a win.

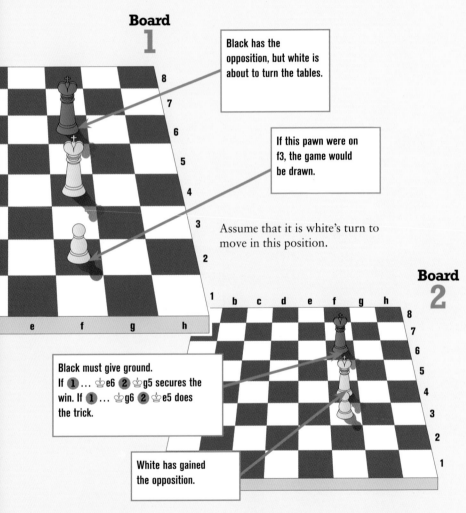

Board 1

Black has the opposition, but white is about to turn the tables.

If this pawn were on f3, the game would be drawn.

Assume that it is white's turn to move in this position.

Board 2

Black must give ground. If **1** ... ♚e6 **2** ♚g5 secures the win. If **1** ... ♚g6 **2** ♚e5 does the trick.

White has gained the opposition.

White simply plays: **1** f3.

Triangulation

Triangulation Triangulation is useful in pawn endings when it is your turn to move, but you don't want to move. Unlike other phases of the game, endings sometimes require you to essentially pass the move in order to make progress. Triangulation is a king maneuver that accomplishes this loss of time.

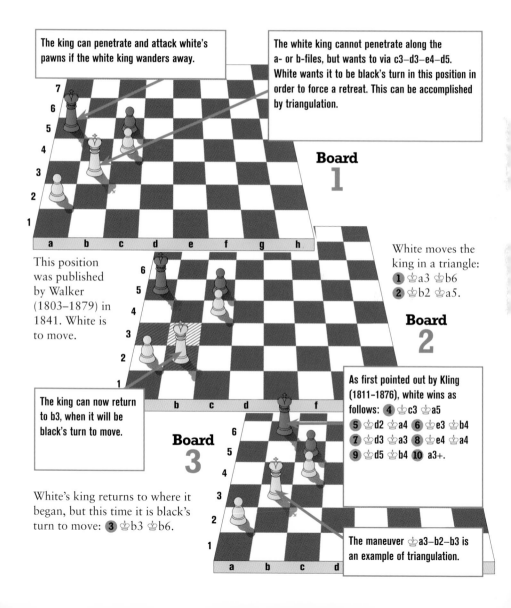

The king can penetrate and attack white's pawns if the white king wanders away.

The white king cannot penetrate along the a- or b-files, but wants to via c3–d3–e4–d5. White wants it to be black's turn in this position in order to force a retreat. This can be accomplished by triangulation.

Board 1

This position was published by Walker (1803–1879) in 1841. White is to move.

White moves the king in a triangle:
1 ♔a3 ♚b6
2 ♔b2 ♚a5.

Board 2

The king can now return to b3, when it will be black's turn to move.

White's king returns to where it began, but this time it is black's turn to move: **3** ♔b3 ♚b6.

Board 3

As first pointed out by Kling (1811–1876), white wins as follows: **4** ♔c3 ♚a5 **5** ♔d2 ♚a4 **6** ♔e3 ♚b4 **7** ♔d3 ♚a3 **8** ♔e4 ♚a4 **9** ♔d5 ♚b4 **10** a3+.

The maneuver ♔a3–b2–b3 is an example of triangulation.

Major Piece Endings

The queen and rook are called *major pieces*, because of their considerable power. These endings can be especially difficult to play correctly. You not only have to worry about a pawn promotion changing the material balance, but also about king safety.

Queen Endings The queen is such a powerful piece that these endings are sometimes decided by brute force. Since there is more open space in general in the endgame and less danger of capture, the queen has tremendous mobility. The defending side will often look for the possibility of perpetual check (☛ see Draw p.19).

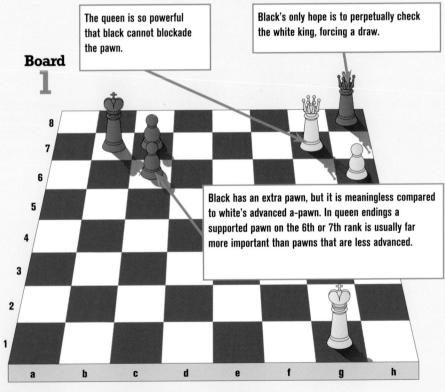

The queen is so powerful that black cannot blockade the pawn.

Black's only hope is to perpetually check the white king, forcing a draw.

Board 1

Black has an extra pawn, but it is meaningless compared to white's advanced a-pawn. In queen endings a supported pawn on the 6th or 7th rank is usually far more important than pawns that are less advanced.

Example 1: In this position it is black's turn to move.

Black's only hope is to keep the white king in perpetual check.

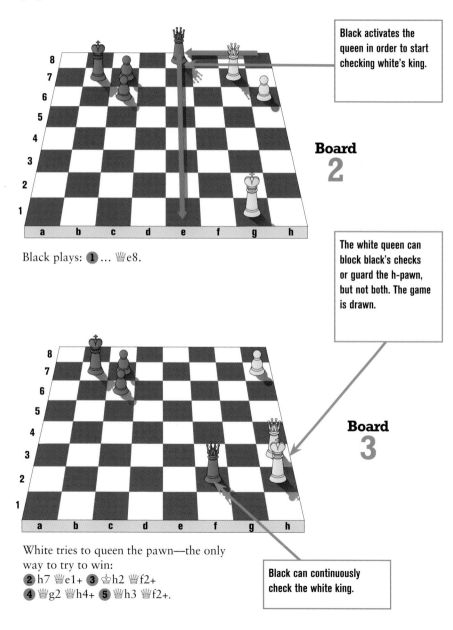

Black plays: **1** ... ♛e8.

White tries to queen the pawn—the only way to try to win:
2 h7 ♛e1+ **3** ♔h2 ♛f2+
4 ♛g2 ♛h4+ **5** ♛h3 ♛f2+.

Board
2

Black activates the queen in order to start checking white's king.

Board
3

The white queen can block black's checks or guard the h-pawn, but not both. The game is drawn.

Black can continuously check the white king.

Queen Endings continued

In general, the stronger side's winning strategy is to trade queens under favorable conditions and transpose into a won pawn ending.

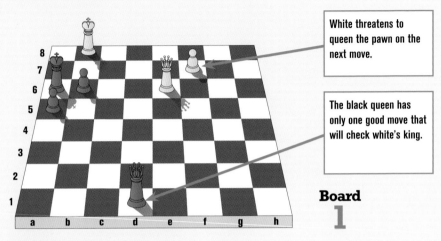

White threatens to queen the pawn on the next move.

The black queen has only one good move that will check white's king.

Board 1

Example 2: Here it is black's turn to move.

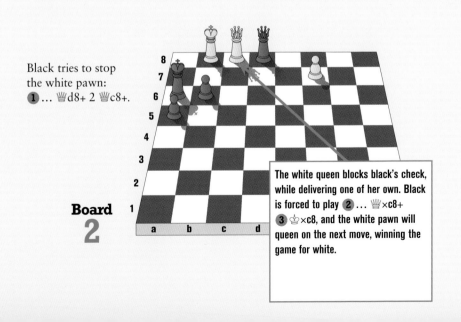

Black tries to stop the white pawn:
1 ... ♛d8+ 2 ♛c8+.

Board 2

The white queen blocks black's check, while delivering one of her own. Black is forced to play 2 ... ♛×c8+ 3 ♚×c8, and the white pawn will queen on the next move, winning the game for white.

Queen Versus Pawn on the 7th Rank

This is an important endgame position to understand completely, because games sometimes boil down to a pawn race for their respective queening squares. If one side queens, and the other makes it only to the 7th rank, what is the result? The answer is that it depends!

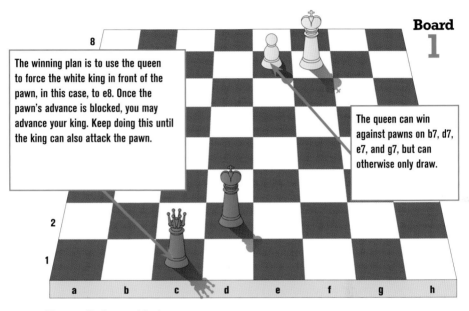

Board 1

The winning plan is to use the queen to force the white king in front of the pawn, in this case, to e8. Once the pawn's advance is blocked, you may advance your king. Keep doing this until the king can also attack the pawn.

The queen can win against pawns on b7, d7, e7, and g7, but can otherwise only draw.

Example 1: It is black's turn to move.

Board 2

A key winning maneuver is to pin the pawn to the king in order to prevent its advance.

White must defend the pawn with the king and try not to get in its way.

Black begins with: **1** ... ♛c7.

Queen Versus Pawn on the 7th Rank continued

From Board 2 play continues:

2 ♔f8 ♕d6 **3** ♔f7 ♕d7 **4** ♔f8 ♕f5+
5 ♔g7 ♕e6 **6** ♔f8 ♕f6+.

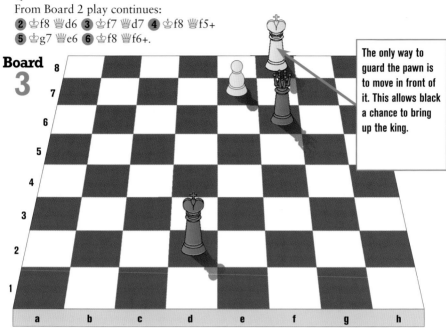

Board 3

The only way to guard the pawn is to move in front of it. This allows black a chance to bring up the king.

Play continues: **7** ♔e8 ♔d3.

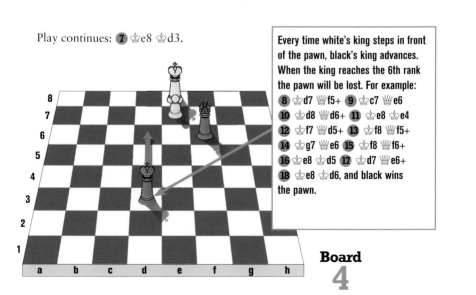

Board 4

Every time white's king steps in front of the pawn, black's king advances. When the king reaches the 6th rank the pawn will be lost. For example:

8 ♔d7 ♕f5+ **9** ♔c7 ♕e6
10 ♔d8 ♕d6+ **11** ♔e8 ♔e4
12 ♔f7 ♕d5+ **13** ♔f8 ♕f5+
14 ♔g7 ♕e6 **15** ♔f8 ♕f6+
16 ♔e8 ♔d5 **17** ♔d7 ♕e6+
18 ♔e8 ♔d6, and black wins the pawn.

Example 2: If the pawn is on either the c-file or the f-file, the game is a draw. The defender has an additional trick up the sleeve, by using the threat of stalemate.

In Board 1 the white king is in check, but this time it doesn't have to protect the pawn.

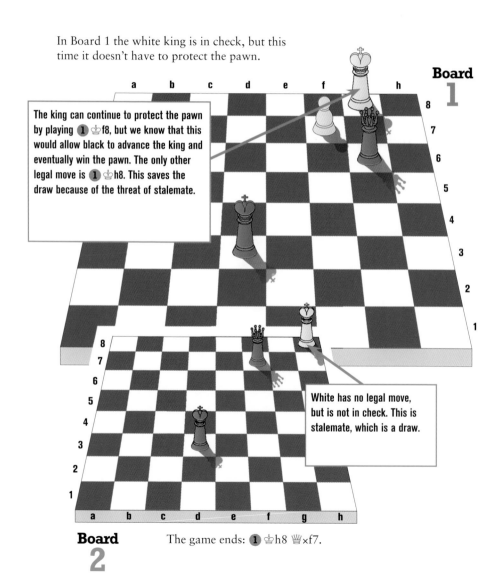

Board 1

The king can continue to protect the pawn by playing ① ♔f8, but we know that this would allow black to advance the king and eventually win the pawn. The only other legal move is ① ♔h8. This saves the draw because of the threat of stalemate.

White has no legal move, but is not in check. This is stalemate, which is a draw.

Board 2

The game ends: ① ♔h8 ♕xf7.

Queen Versus Rook The queen is considerably more powerful than the rook. If there are no pawns involved, the winning strategy is to separate the king and rook, and pick off the rook with check. Sometimes you can use the threat of checkmate in order to win the rook.

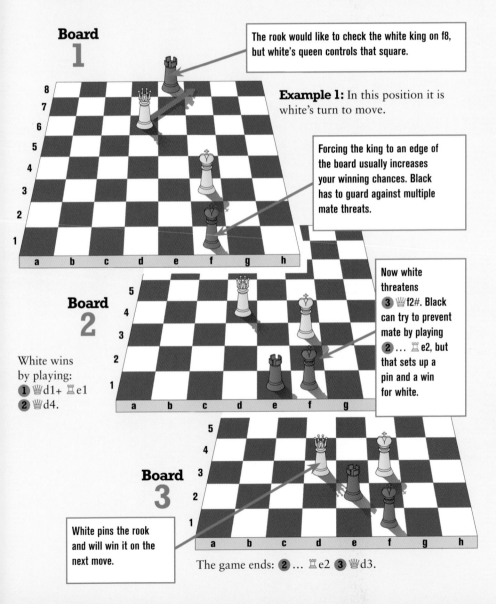

Board 1

The rook would like to check the white king on f8, but white's queen controls that square.

Example 1: In this position it is white's turn to move.

Forcing the king to an edge of the board usually increases your winning chances. Black has to guard against multiple mate threats.

Board 2

White wins by playing:
① ♕d1+ ♖e1
② ♕d4.

Now white threatens ③ ♕f2#. Black can try to prevent mate by playing ② ... ♖e2, but that sets up a pin and a win for white.

Board 3

White pins the rook and will win it on the next move.

The game ends: ② ... ♖e2 ③ ♕d3.

Example 2: If pawns are involved the defending side can sometimes establish what is known as a *fortress*. A fortress is an unassailable position, where the stronger side is unable to break down the weaker side's defenses. The result is a draw.

As long as the rook remains on the 5th rank the white king cannot help the queen.

The queen cannot penetrate along the 8th rank or the h-file. Its only avenue of attack is along the g-file.

The rook can simply move back and forth between e5 and g5. White cannot make any progress.

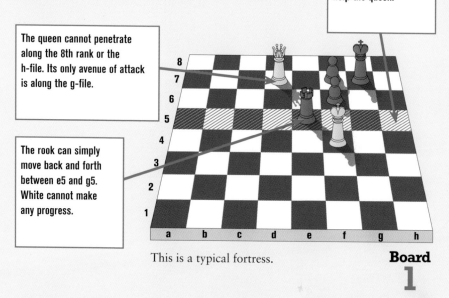

This is a typical fortress.

Board
1

The rook can always block the queen's checks along the g-file and force the queen to retreat. Once the queen moves away, the rook simply returns to e5. The game is drawn.

Board
2

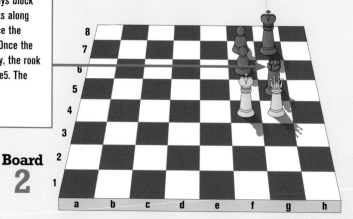

White can try to invade along the g-file: ① ♕g4+ ♖g5, but it is to no avail.

Rook Versus Pawn Rook versus pawn is an obvious mismatch except when the weaker side's king is active, and the stronger side's is not. A rook is much less mobile than the queen and can usually only draw if the pawn reaches the 7th rank. If the pawn is less advanced, the rook may prove decisive if it can trap the enemy king far enough back.

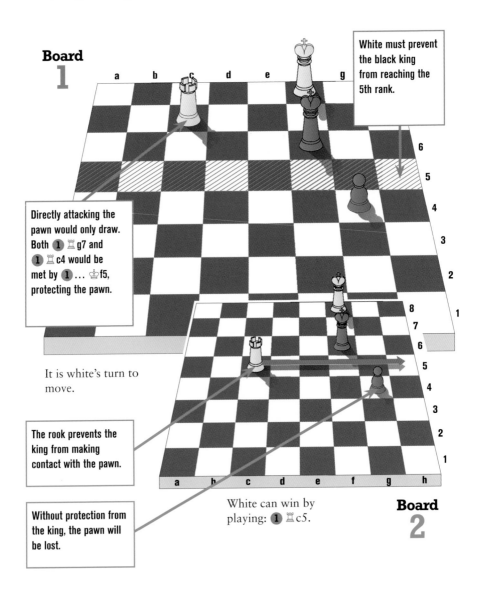

Board 1

White must prevent the black king from reaching the 5th rank.

Directly attacking the pawn would only draw. Both **1** ♖g7 and **1** ♖c4 would be met by **1** ... ♚f5, protecting the pawn.

It is white's turn to move.

The rook prevents the king from making contact with the pawn.

Without protection from the king, the pawn will be lost.

White can win by playing: **1** ♖c5.

Board 2

Once the king is cut off from the pawn before it reaches the 5th rank, the rook can prevent the pawn from queening. If black does not advance the pawn, the white king will slowly but surely march up and around and win the pawn.

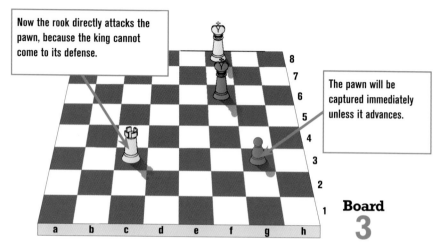

Now the rook directly attacks the pawn, because the king cannot come to its defense.

The pawn will be captured immediately unless it advances.

Board 3

Black therefore has to try to promote the pawn:
1 ... g3 **2** ♖c3.

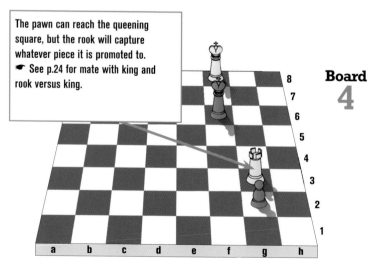

The pawn can reach the queening square, but the rook will capture whatever piece it is promoted to.
☞ See p.24 for mate with king and rook versus king.

Board 4

The pawn tries to escape: **2** ... g2 **3** ♖g3.

The Saavedra Position This is one of the most celebrated chess compositions, first published in 1895. It is a startling example of how a single pawn can defeat a lone rook.

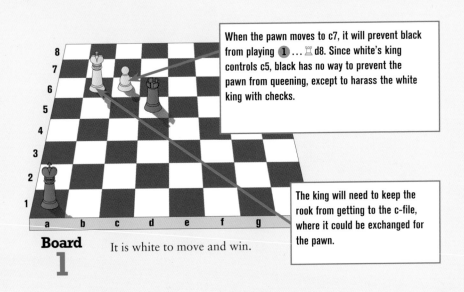

When the pawn moves to c7, it will prevent black from playing **①** ... ♖d8. Since white's king controls c5, black has no way to prevent the pawn from queening, except to harass the white king with checks.

The king will need to keep the rook from getting to the c-file, where it could be exchanged for the pawn.

Board 1

It is white to move and win.

Board 2

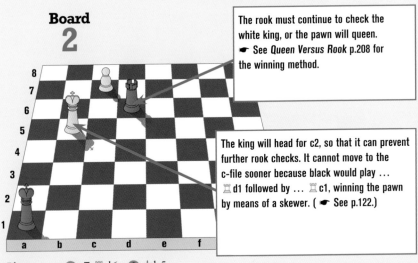

The rook must continue to check the white king, or the pawn will queen. ☛ See *Queen Versus Rook* p.208 for the winning method.

The king will head for c2, so that it can prevent further rook checks. It cannot move to the c-file sooner because black would play ... ♖d1 followed by ... ♖c1, winning the pawn by means of a skewer. (☛ See p.122.)

Play starts: **①** c7 ♖d6+ **②** ♔b5.

Black still has one more trick to play.

Board 3

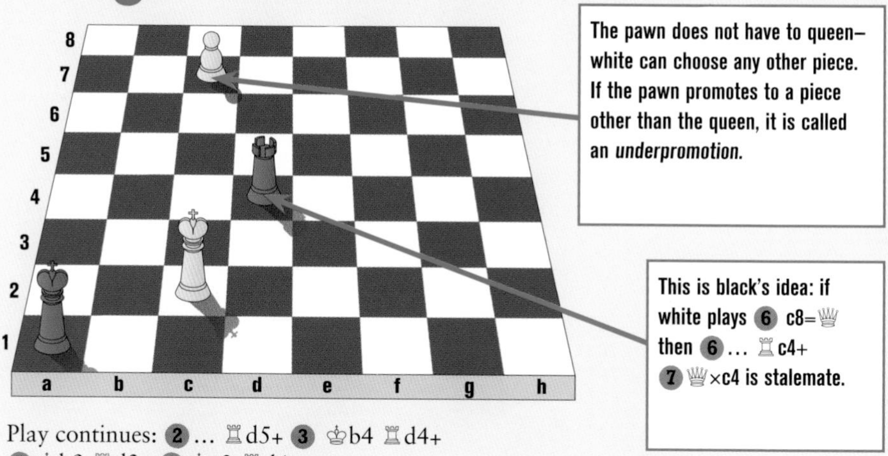

The pawn does not have to queen— white can choose any other piece. If the pawn promotes to a piece other than the queen, it is called an *underpromotion*.

This is black's idea: if white plays **6** c8=♕ then **6** ... ♖c4+ **7** ♕×c4 is stalemate.

Play continues: **2** ... ♖d5+ **3** ♔b4 ♖d4+ **4** ♔b3 ♖d3+ **5** ♔c2 ♖d4.

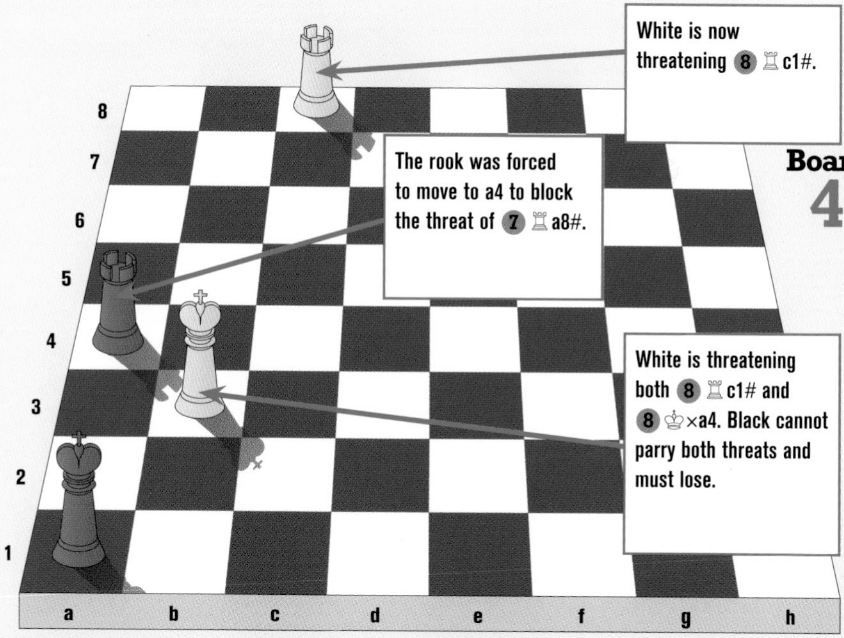

White is now threatening **8** ♖c1#.

Board 4

The rook was forced to move to a4 to block the threat of **7** ♖a8#.

White is threatening both **8** ♖c1# and **8** ♔×a4. Black cannot parry both threats and must lose.

White wins by underpromoting to a rook: **6** c8=♖ ♖a4 **7** ♔b3.

Rook Versus Two Connected Pawns It is remarkable that this ending also has practical value. If you play enough chess, you'll run into this situation in one of your games eventually. The rule of thumb is that the pawns win if they reach the 6th rank.

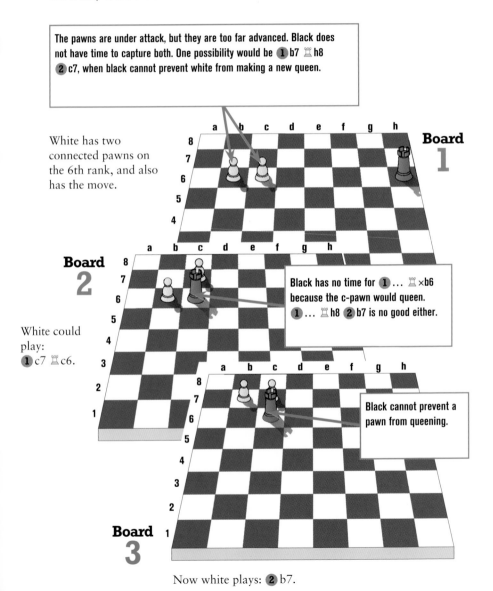

The pawns are under attack, but they are too far advanced. Black does not have time to capture both. One possibility would be **1** b7 ♜ h8 **2** c7, when black cannot prevent white from making a new queen.

White has two connected pawns on the 6th rank, and also has the move.

Board 1

Board 2

Black has no time for **1** … ♜ ×b6 because the c-pawn would queen. **1** … ♜ h8 **2** b7 is no good either.

White could play: **1** c7 ♜ c6.

Black cannot prevent a pawn from queening.

Board 3

Now white plays: **2** b7.

Rook and Pawn Endings

If you reach an ending, it will probably be a rook and pawn ending (usually just called *rook endings*). Rook endings occur about as often as all other endings combined. A small advantage in these endings is difficult to convert into a win, which has led to the half-serious claim that all rook endings are drawn.

Rook and Pawn Versus Rook These are most often won when the defender's king is cut off from the queening square. If the king can reach the queening square the win is more difficult, and in some cases impossible. The following diagrams show what may happen when the pawn reaches the 6th rank.

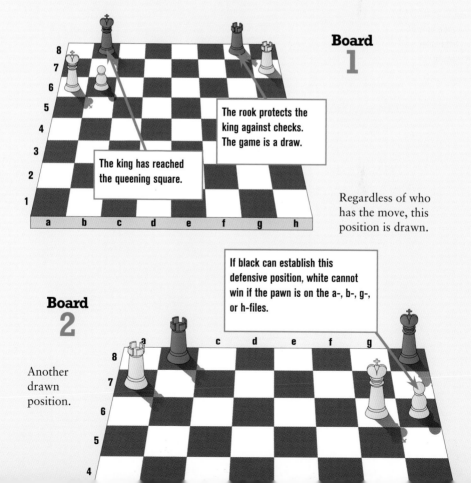

Board 1

The rook protects the king against checks. The game is a draw.

The king has reached the queening square.

Regardless of who has the move, this position is drawn.

If black can establish this defensive position, white cannot win if the pawn is on the a-, b-, g-, or h-files.

Board 2

Another drawn position.

Rook and Pawn Versus Rook continued

Example 3: If the pawn is on the center files (c-, d-, e-, or f-files), the side with the pawn can win.

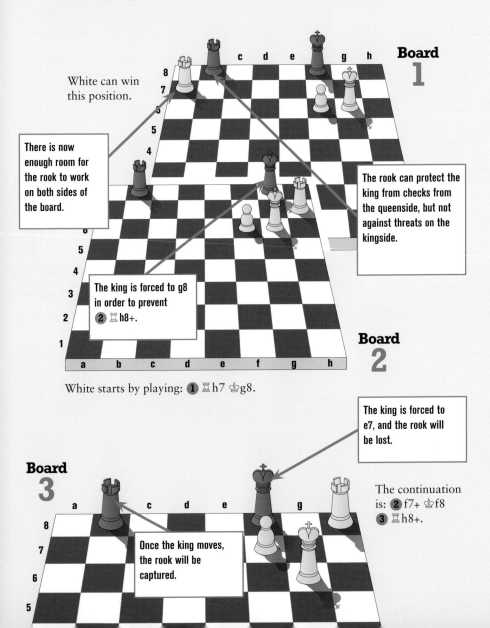

Board **1**

White can win this position.

There is now enough room for the rook to work on both sides of the board.

The rook can protect the king from checks from the queenside, but not against threats on the kingside.

The king is forced to g8 in order to prevent **2** ♖h8+.

White starts by playing: **1** ♖h7 ♔g8.

Board **2**

The king is forced to e7, and the rook will be lost.

Board **3**

Once the king moves, the rook will be captured.

The continuation is: **2** f7+ ♔f8 **3** ♖h8+.

Philidor's Position If the pawn has not yet reached the 6th rank, and the stronger side has a less favorable king position, it may prove impossible to win. Philidor demonstrated the drawing technique back in the eighteenth century.

The king has been able to occupy the queening square.

The pawn has yet to reach the 6th rank.

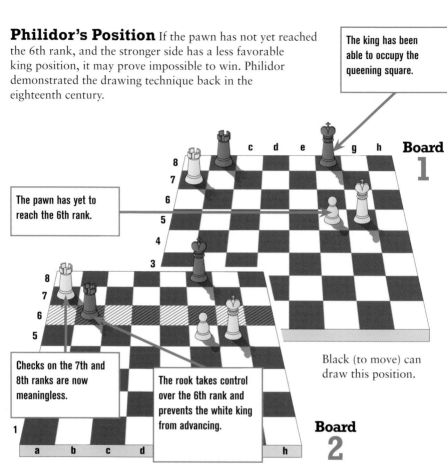

Board 1

Black (to move) can draw this position.

Checks on the 7th and 8th ranks are now meaningless.

The rook takes control over the 6th rank and prevents the white king from advancing.

Board 2

Black must play ❶ ... ♖b6.

Once the pawn has advanced, it can no longer effectively shield the king from harassing checks.

Board 3

The only way for white to make progress is to play ❷ f6.

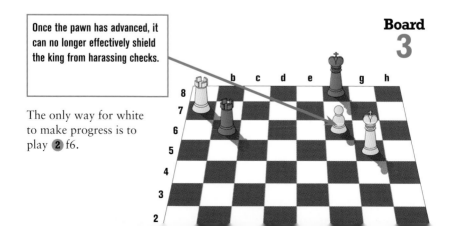

Philidor's Position continued

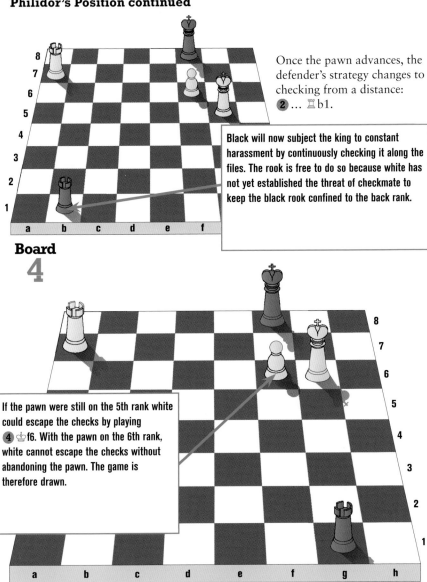

Once the pawn advances, the defender's strategy changes to checking from a distance:
2 ... ♖b1.

Black will now subject the king to constant harassment by continuously checking it along the files. The rook is free to do so because white has not yet established the threat of checkmate to keep the black rook confined to the back rank.

Board 4

If the pawn were still on the 5th rank white could escape the checks by playing **4** ♔f6. With the pawn on the 6th rank, white cannot escape the checks without abandoning the pawn. The game is therefore drawn.

White threatens checkmate, but black defends by giving check:
3 ♔g6 ♖g1+.

Board 5

Lucena's Position
This is one of the best-known endgame positions. It illustrates the winning method in the following type of position.

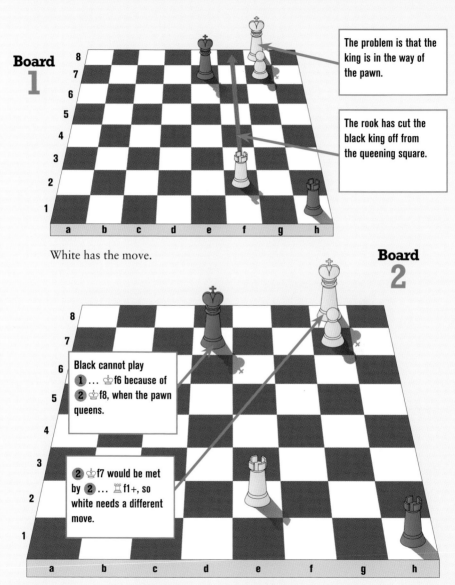

Board 1

The problem is that the king is in the way of the pawn.

The rook has cut the black king off from the queening square.

White has the move.

Board 2

Black cannot play ❶ ... ♔f6 because of ❷ ♔f8, when the pawn queens.

❷ ♔f7 would be met by ❷ ... ♖f1+, so white needs a different move.

White begins by forcing the black king to move further away from the pawn: ❶ ♖e2+ ♔d7.

Lucena's Position continued

Board 3

An odd looking move, but ② ♖e4 is the key to winning the game. The rook will be used as a blocker to stop black's checks. The maneuver is referred to as *building a bridge*.

White now plays:
② ♖e4.

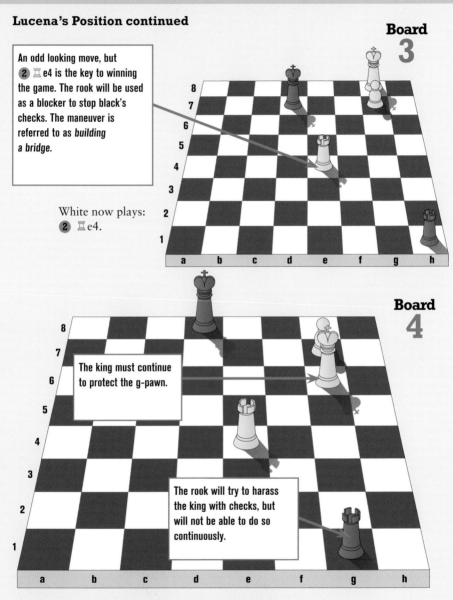

Board 4

The king must continue to protect the g-pawn.

The rook will try to harass the king with checks, but will not be able to do so continuously.

Play continues: ② ... ♔d8 ③ ♔f7 ♖f1+ ④ ♔g6 ♖g1+.

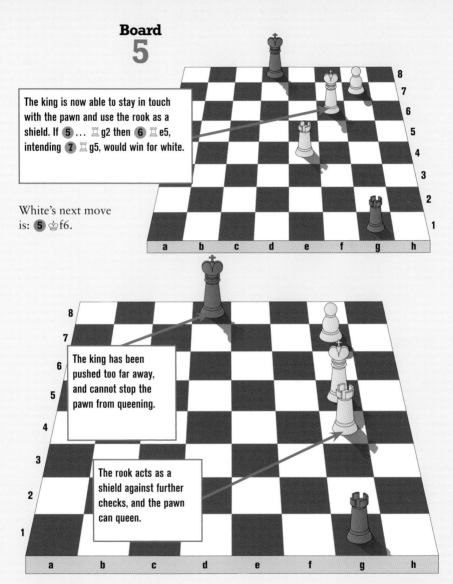

Board 5

The king is now able to stay in touch with the pawn and use the rook as a shield. If **5** ... ♖g2 then **6** ♖e5, intending **7** ♖g5, would win for white.

White's next move is: **5** ♔f6.

The king has been pushed too far away, and cannot stop the pawn from queening.

The rook acts as a shield against further checks, and the pawn can queen.

Black tries to keep checking: **5** ... ♖f1+ **6** ♔g5 ♖g1+ **7** ♖g4.

Board 6

Long Side Checking Once you understand the defensive technique of distance checking along the files (☛ see Philidor's Position p.217), it is a short step to realizing that checking along the ranks might accomplish the same end. The important thing to remember is the rook belongs on the long side of the board.

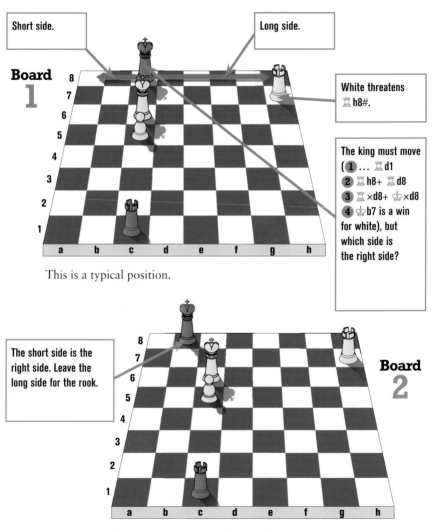

Short side.

Long side.

Board 1

White threatens ♖h8#.

The king must move (**1** ... ♖d1 **2** ♖h8+ ♖d8 **3** ♖×d8+ ♔×d8 **4** ♔b7 is a win for white), but which side is the right side?

This is a typical position.

The short side is the right side. Leave the long side for the rook.

Board 2

The correct move is: **1** ... ♔b8.

The rook can use the long side to check the white king away
from the action. The black king remains close enough to lend
a hand when needed.

Board
3

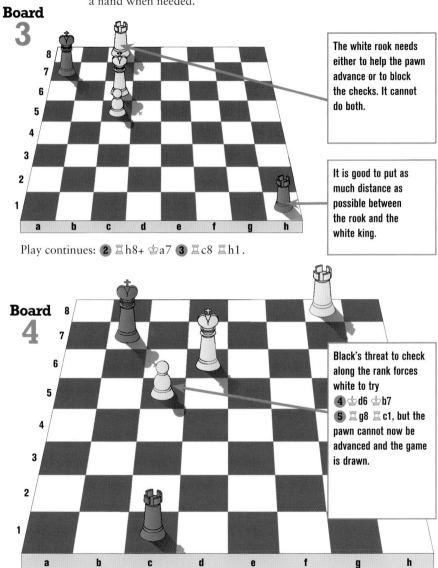

The white rook needs
either to help the pawn
advance or to block
the checks. It cannot
do both.

It is good to put as
much distance as
possible between
the rook and the
white king.

Play continues: **2** ♖h8+ ♚a7 **3** ♖c8 ♖h1.

Board
4

Black's threat to check
along the rank forces
white to try
4 ♚d6 ♚b7
5 ♖g8 ♖c1, but the
pawn cannot now be
advanced and the game
is drawn.

After **5** ♖g7+ ♚c8 **6** ♚c6 ♚b8 (short side) white has made no progress.

Pawn On The 7th "Rooks belong behind passed pawns," goes the old saying, whether one's own or the opponent's. Trying to stop a pawn on the 7th from the side or the front is usually a mistake. Even when your rook is behind the pawn there are some tricks to contend with.

Attacking the pawn from the side isn't the best strategy.

Example 1: Here is a typical position.

Board 1

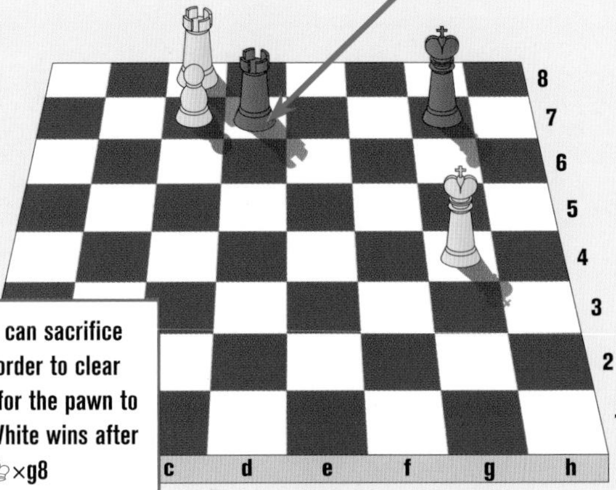

8
7
6
5
4
3
2
1

c   d   e   f   g   h

The rook can sacrifice itself in order to clear the way for the pawn to queen. White wins after

1 ... ♚×g8
2 c8=♕+ and
3 ♕×d7.

Board 2

a   b   c   e   f   h

8
7
6
5
4
3
2

White plays:
1 ♖g8+.

Example 2: It is a different story when the rook is attacking the pawn from behind.

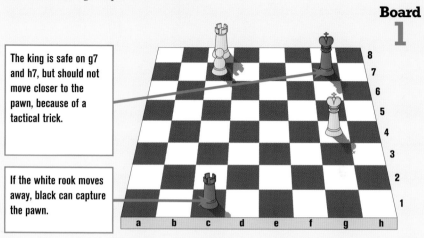

The king is safe on g7 and h7, but should not move closer to the pawn, because of a tactical trick.

If the white rook moves away, black can capture the pawn.

Attempting to approach the pawn with the king would be a blunder:
1 ... ♔f7? **2** ♖h8.

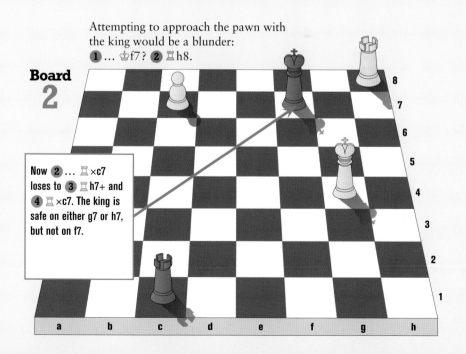

Now **2** ... ♖×c7 loses to **3** ♖h7+ and **4** ♖×c7. The king is safe on either g7 or h7, but not on f7.

Pawn On The 7th continued

If the black king oscillates between g7 and h7 white cannot make any progress. White can try to defend the pawn with the king, but then the king is exposed to check.

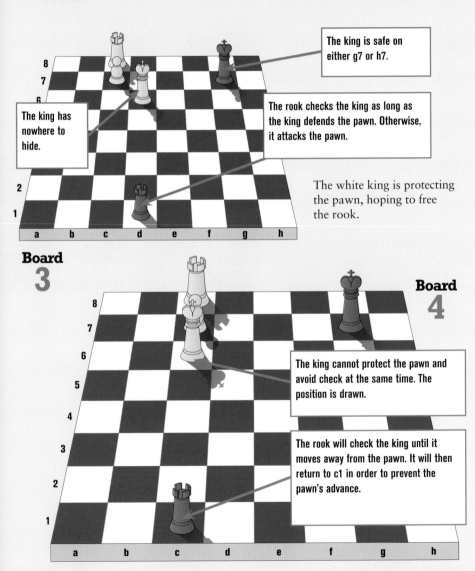

The king is safe on either g7 or h7.

The king has nowhere to hide.

The rook checks the king as long as the king defends the pawn. Otherwise, it attacks the pawn.

The white king is protecting the pawn, hoping to free the rook.

Board 3

Board 4

The king cannot protect the pawn and avoid check at the same time. The position is drawn.

The rook will check the king until it moves away from the pawn. It will then return to c1 in order to prevent the pawn's advance.

Play continues: ❶ ♔c6 ♖c1+.

Rook and Multiple Pawns The more pawns there are on the board the greater the winning chances. Sometimes the combination of active rook and superior king position can turn a game which looks like a draw into a win. This is a position from Rubinstein–Alekhine, Karlsbad 1911.

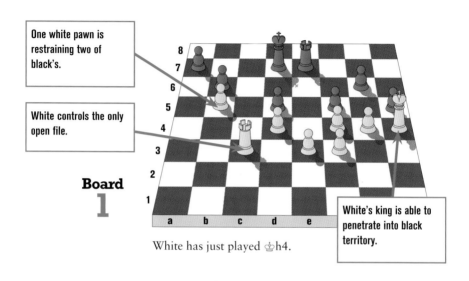

One white pawn is restraining two of black's.

White controls the only open file.

White's king is able to penetrate into black territory.

White has just played ♔h4.

Board 1

Board 2

Black cannot defend this pawn, and ended up losing the game.

The game continued:
1 ... ♖h7
2 ♔g5 fxg4
3 fxg4 hxg4
4 ♔xg4.

Rook and Multiple Pawns continued

An active rook is much better than a passive one, even if it costs you a pawn to make the rook active. That is what black did in the famous game Tarrasch–Rubinstein, San Sebastian 1911.

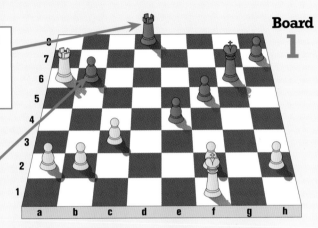

The rook can take on the role of passive defender, or it can turn into an aggressive attacker.

Black is already a pawn down, and another one is under attack. Passive defense by **1** ... ♖d6 would be insufficient.

Board 1

White has just played ♖a6, attacking the b-pawn.

Board 2

From here the rook can attack white's pawns, and give the white king some grief.

Black activates the rook: **1** ... ♖d2.

Black uses the active rook and superior king position to create serious threats against white's position. This forces a simplification of the position, which reduces white's winning chances.

Board 3

Black is threatening ⑤ ... f4 and ⑥ ... ♔f3 when white would be in serious trouble.

The game continued: ② ♖×b6+ ♔g5 ③ ♔e1 ♖c2 ④ ♖b5 ♔g4.

White's advantage has been reduced to a single pawn which is not very far advanced. The game was soon agreed drawn.

Board 4

White dealt with the threat to his king by playing:
⑤ h3+ ♔×h3 ⑥ ♖×f5 ♖×b2 ⑦ ♖f4 ♖×a2 ⑧ ♖×e4 h5.

Bishop Endings

Bishops are most effective in open positions. The reduction in material that characterizes endings usually plays right into the bishop's hands. The bishop's main drawback is that it moves on either light or dark squares, but not both. Color matters more in bishop endings than any other type.

Bishop Versus Pawns A bishop is adept at stopping a single passed pawn. It can stop two pawns with the help of its king. The bishop can hold the game without the king's help if it can stop the pawns along a single diagonal.

The bishop is able to prevent the advance of either pawn.

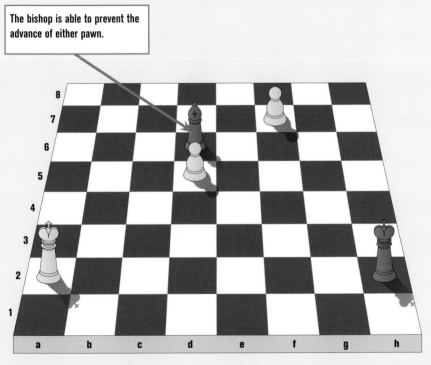

This position is drawn.

If the bishop must use two different diagonals in order to stop the pawns, it may be possible to sacrifice one and queen the other. The bishop's task is more difficult the further apart and the further advanced the pawns are.

The bishop can capture either pawn, if they advance, but it cannot stop them both.

1 b6 ♗×b6
2 e7 when the pawn queens.

Board 1

This position is a win for white.

White wins after: **1** b6 ♗d6 **2** b7.

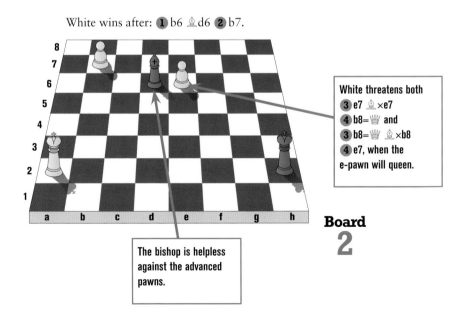

White threatens both
3 e7 ♗×e7
4 b8=♕ and
3 b8=♕ ♗×b8
4 e7, when the e-pawn will queen.

Board 2

The bishop is helpless against the advanced pawns.

Bishop Versus Pawns continued

Three pawns will usually defeat a bishop, unless the bishop can blockade or capture them.

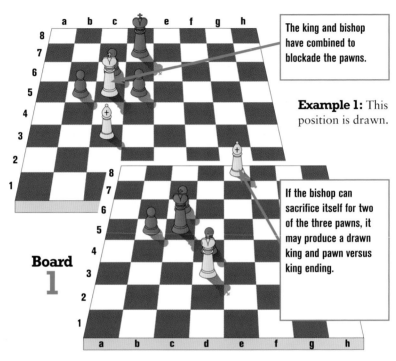

The king and bishop have combined to blockade the pawns.

Example 1: This position is drawn.

If the bishop can sacrifice itself for two of the three pawns, it may produce a drawn king and pawn versus king ending.

Board 1

Example 2: White can draw this position.

Board 2

White plays:
1 ♗xc6 ♚xc6
2 ♚xd4.

The king can prevent the pawn from queening and the game is drawn.

The Wrong Bishop

It would seem that a bishop and pawn could always win against a lone king, but there is one set of positions in which they cannot. If the bishop cannot control a rook pawn's queening square, it may be impossible to win the game.

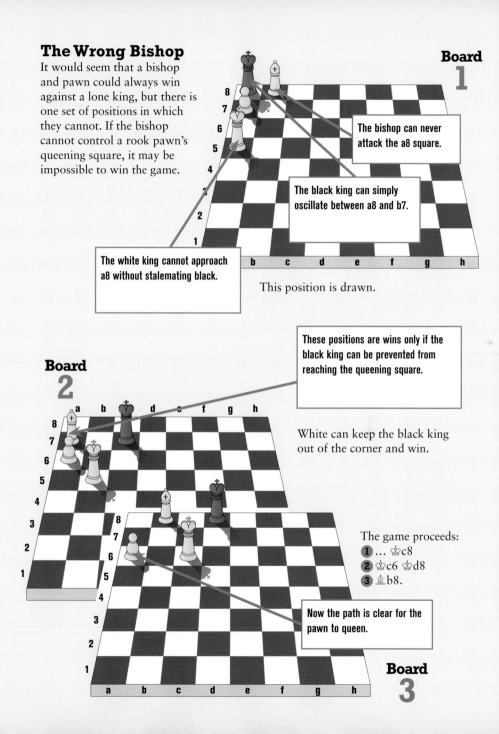

The bishop can never attack the a8 square.

The black king can simply oscillate between a8 and b7.

The white king cannot approach a8 without stalemating black.

This position is drawn.

These positions are wins only if the black king can be prevented from reaching the queening square.

White can keep the black king out of the corner and win.

The game proceeds:
1 ... ♚c8
2 ♔c6 ♚d8
3 ♗b8.

Now the path is clear for the pawn to queen.

Same Color Bishops These endings occur when both sides have a bishop confined to the same color. As usual, winning chances increase along with the number of pawns. A bishop and pawn can defeat a bishop only under special circumstances. Below is a composition by Centurini from 1856.

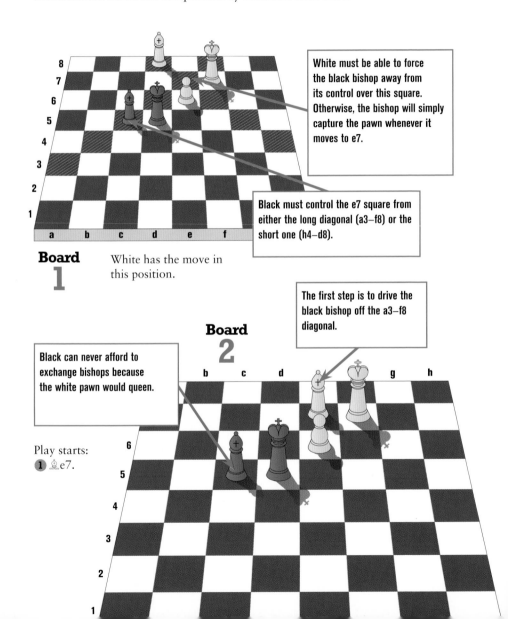

White must be able to force the black bishop away from its control over this square. Otherwise, the bishop will simply capture the pawn whenever it moves to e7.

Black must control the e7 square from either the long diagonal (a3–f8) or the short one (h4–d8).

Board 1

White has the move in this position.

The first step is to drive the black bishop off the a3–f8 diagonal.

Black can never afford to exchange bishops because the white pawn would queen.

Board 2

Play starts:
1 ♗e7.

Once the black bishop is forced off the long diagonal, it must head for the short one.

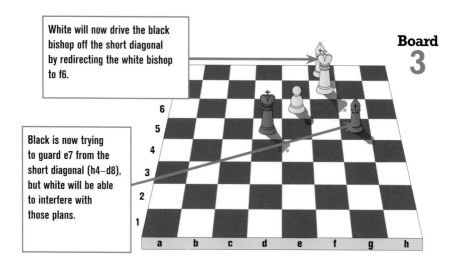

White will now drive the black bishop off the short diagonal by redirecting the white bishop to f6.

Black is now trying to guard e7 from the short diagonal (h4–d8), but white will be able to interfere with those plans.

Board 3

Play continues: **1** ... ♗e3 **2** ♗f8 ♗g5.

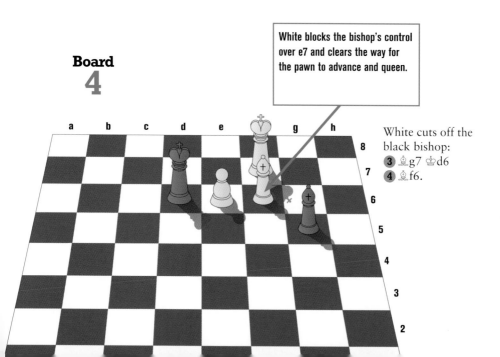

Board 4

White blocks the bishop's control over e7 and clears the way for the pawn to advance and queen.

White cuts off the black bishop:
3 ♗g7 ♔d6
4 ♗f6.

Same Color Bishops continued

When there are multiple pawns per side you want to place your pawns on the opposite color from the bishop. The following position arose in the game Polugayevsky–Mecking, Mar del Plata 1971.

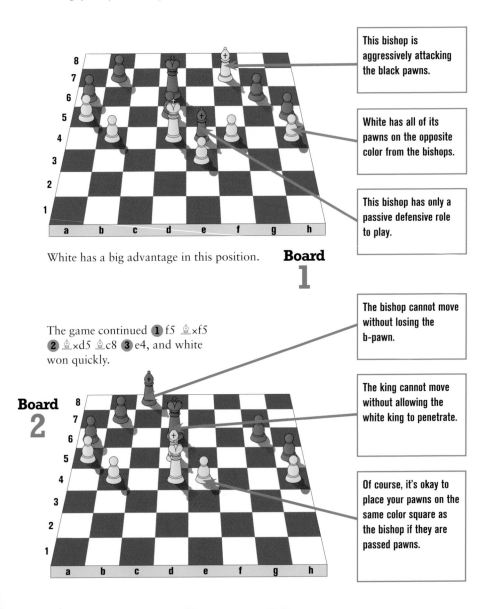

This bishop is aggressively attacking the black pawns.

White has all of its pawns on the opposite color from the bishops.

This bishop has only a passive defensive role to play.

White has a big advantage in this position.

Board 1

The game continued **1** f5 ♗xf5 **2** ♗xd5 ♗c8 **3** e4, and white won quickly.

Board 2

The bishop cannot move without losing the b-pawn.

The king cannot move without allowing the white king to penetrate.

Of course, it's okay to place your pawns on the same color square as the bishop if they are passed pawns.

Opposite Color Bishops

These endings tend to end in draws, simply because the bishops can never oppose one another. You still want to put your pawns on the opposite color from your bishop, unless you are trying to establish a blockade.

> Black has two additional pawns, but they are hopelessly blockaded. The position is drawn.

Example 1: A typical blockade.

Board

1

> Even two extra connected passed pawns may not be enough to win, if the defender can blockade them.

> The bishop simply stays on the h4–d8 diagonal and prevents black's pawns from advancing.

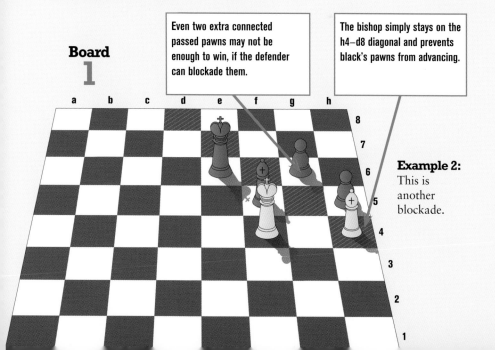

Example 2: This is another blockade.

Opposite Color Bishops continued

In the absence of a blockade a two-pawn advantage is often enough to win. The winning chances are greater when the pawns are on opposite wings.

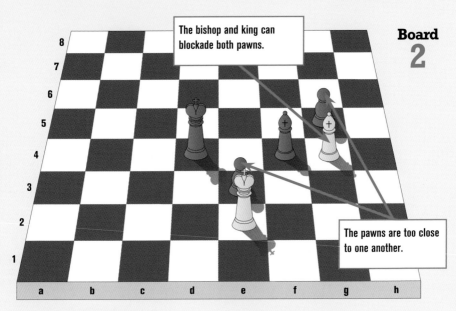

The bishop and king can blockade both pawns.

Board 2

The pawns are too close to one another.

This position is drawn.

Board 3

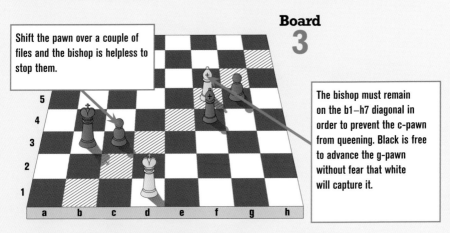

Shift the pawn over a couple of files and the bishop is helpless to stop them.

The bishop must remain on the b1–h7 diagonal in order to prevent the c-pawn from queening. Black is free to advance the g-pawn without fear that white will capture it.

However, in this position black wins.

Knight Endings

The knight is an exceptional piece in more ways than one. Its eccentricities of movement can lead to many surprising twists and turns. Its main weakness in the ending is its inability to cover both sides of the board simultaneously.

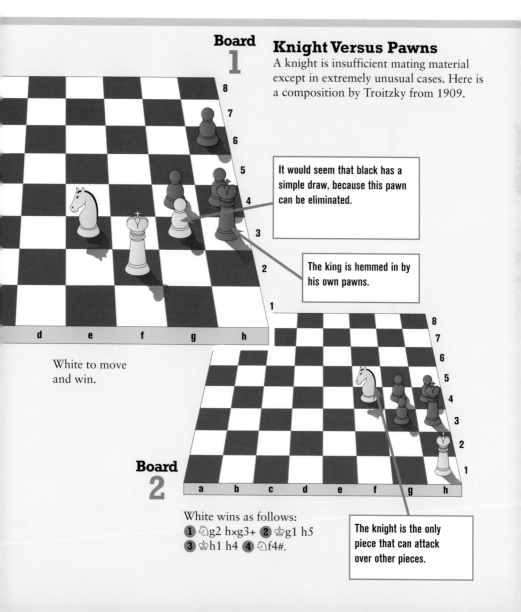

Knight Versus Pawns

Board 1

A knight is insufficient mating material except in extremely unusual cases. Here is a composition by Troitzky from 1909.

It would seem that black has a simple draw, because this pawn can be eliminated.

The king is hemmed in by his own pawns.

White to move and win.

Board 2

White wins as follows:
1 ♘g2 h×g3+ **2** ♔g1 h5
3 ♔h1 h4 **4** ♘f4#.

The knight is the only piece that can attack over other pieces.

Knight Versus Pawn The knight cannot stop a rook pawn on the 7th without the king's help. The drawing technique for knight against other pawns on the 7th is an important one to master.

Once the knight is in front of the pawn, the game is a draw.

Board 1

White to move. The knight blockades the pawn.

If the king moves back to d6, the knight returns to d8. If the king moves anywhere else, the black king can advance toward the pawn.

Board 2

Play commences: **1** ♔c7 ♘e6+.

When white approaches from one side, the knight simply moves to the other.

Board 3

Black continues to blockade the pawn: **2** ♔d6 ♘d8 **3** ♔e7 ♘c6+.

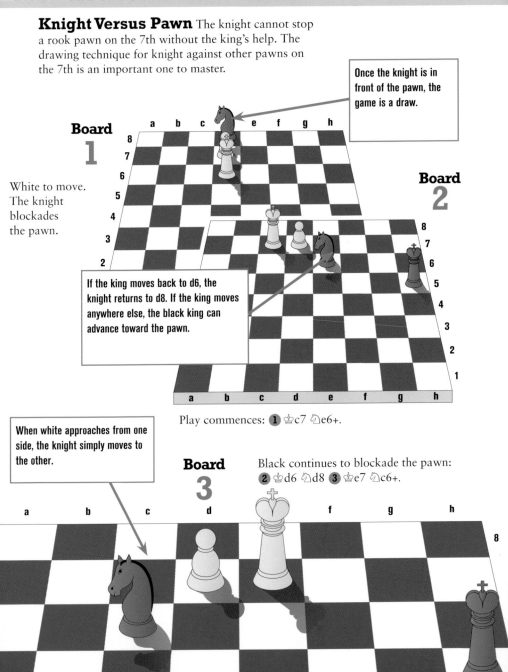

Knight and Pawn

A knight and pawn will always win as long as the pawn can be defended. The knight should defend the pawn from the rear.

Board 1

The knight cannot maintain the defense of the pawn from in front of it. After **1** ... ♔d6, either the knight or the pawn will be lost.

The knight is badly placed here.

Board 2

The knight can defend the pawn from behind it because the black king cannot approach it. **1** ... ♔c4 **2** d6 and the pawn queens.

This is the right place for the knight.

Knight and Rook Pawns There is a special case in which even a knight and protected pawn are insufficient to win.

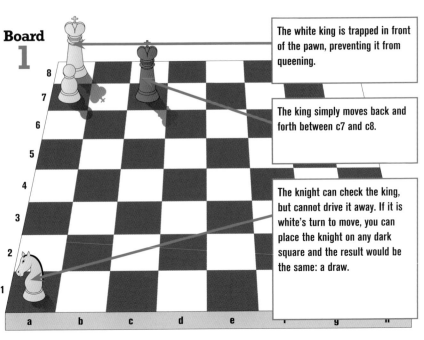

Board 1

The white king is trapped in front of the pawn, preventing it from queening.

The king simply moves back and forth between c7 and c8.

The knight can check the king, but cannot drive it away. If it is white's turn to move, you can place the knight on any dark square and the result would be the same: a draw.

White to move. This position is drawn.

Board 2

Now, it is white to move and win—for example ① ♘g3 ♚c8 ② ♘f5 ♚c7 ③ ♘e7 and the black king cannot move to c8. You may place the knight on any light square (except c8) and it will be white to move and win.

With the knight on a white square, white wins.

Knight and Pawn Versus Knight

The respective king positions determine the outcome in this case. If the defender's king is out of play, the stronger side will usually win. When the stronger side's king is out of play, you usually need a trick in order to win.

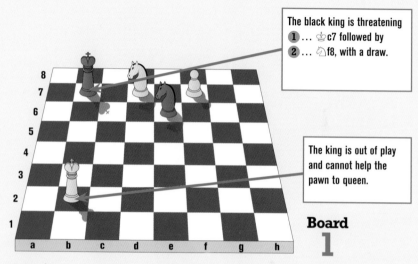

The black king is threatening
1 ... ♚c7 followed by
2 ... ♘f8, with a draw.

The king is out of play and cannot help the pawn to queen.

Board
1

It is white's turn to move in this position.

Board
2

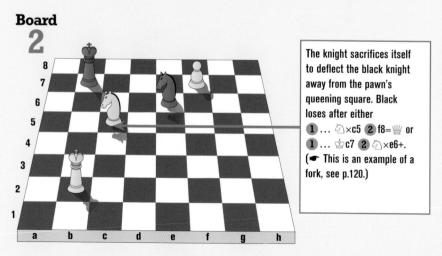

The knight sacrifices itself to deflect the black knight away from the pawn's queening square. Black loses after either
1 ... ♘×c5 **2** f8=♛ or
1 ... ♚c7 **2** ♘×e6+.
(☛ This is an example of a fork, see p.120.)

White wins with a tactical trick: **1** ♘c5+.

Knight and Multiple Pawns
These endings are usually drawn if all the pawns are on the same side of the board. Passed pawns (☞ see p.179), especially outside passed pawns, can be especially effective in these endings.

As with pure pawn endings, the other decisive factor is the position of the kings.

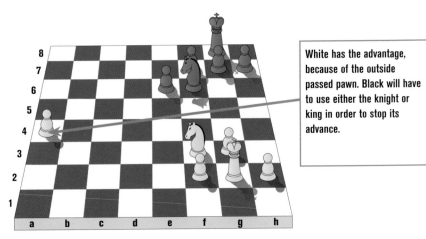

White has the advantage, because of the outside passed pawn. Black will have to use either the knight or king in order to stop its advance.

Example 1: Material is level, but white's passed pawn is significant.

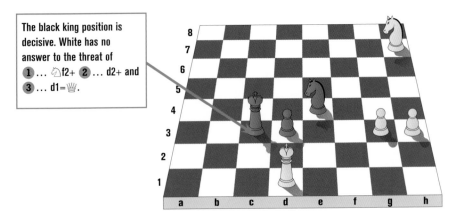

The black king position is decisive. White has no answer to the threat of
1 ... ♘f2+ **2** ... d2+ and
3 ... d1=♕.

Example 2: Black has the move in this position. Even though white has an extra pawn, black can win easily.

Bishop Versus Knight Endings

Knights and bishops have roughly equal powers, but their natures are very different. For example, blocked positions inhibit the bishop's powers, but sometimes magnify the knight's. Open positions with pawns on both sides of the board tend to favor the speedy bishop at the expense of the slower-moving knight.

Knight and Pawn Versus Bishop The bishop can cover so much ground that there aren't too many ways for the stronger side to win these endings. One possibility is to use the knight as a shield.

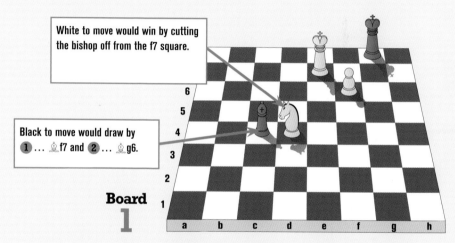

White to move would win by cutting the bishop off from the f7 square.

Black to move would draw by
1 ... ♗f7 and 2 ... ♗g6.

Board 1

In this position, the result depends on whose turn it is to move.

White to move wins by 1 ♘e6.

Board 2

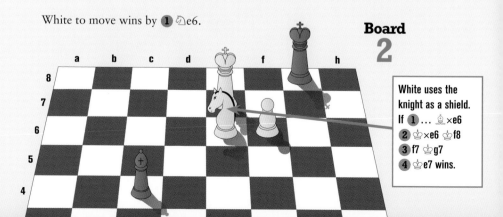

White uses the knight as a shield.
If 1 ... ♗×e6
2 ♔×e6 ♔f8
3 f7 ♔g7
4 ♔e7 wins.

Bishop and Pawn Versus Knight

If the weaker side can establish a blockade, or if the king can control the queening square, then these positions are almost always drawn. The only serious winning chances occur when the defender's pieces are badly placed.

Board

1

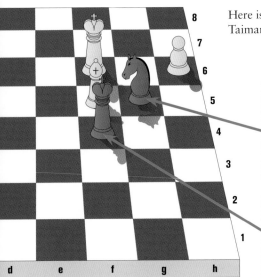

Here is an example from the game Fischer–Taimanov, Vancouver 1971.

> The knight has more trouble with wing pawns than center pawns, because it only has one side on which to maneuver.

> The game would be drawn if the king could reach h8, but it is too far out of play on f4.

> Black is in zugzwang (☞ see p.193). Any move loses, and passing is not allowed!

Board

2

White won by playing: **1** ♔g6.

When The Bishop Is Better

The bishop is almost always better when there are pawns on both sides of the board and chances to create a passed pawn. It is also much easier for the side with the bishop to transpose into a winning king and pawn ending.

The bishop attacks many of the squares the knight would like to move to, either now or later.

Black is threatening to create a passed pawn with ① ... b4. If ② a×b4 a3 white would not be able to prevent the pawn from queening.

Board 1

Here is an example from the game Réti–Rubinstein, Gothenburg 1920.

White tried: ① ♘e4+ ♗×e4 ② d×e4 b4 ③ ♔d2 b×a3 ④ ♔c1 g5.

Black wins after ⑤ f×g5 f×g5 by penetrating with the king via e5 and capturing white's kingside pawns.

Board 2

When The Knight Is Better

The knight is frequently better when the opponent's pawns are on squares of the same color as the bishop. The king is often free to penetrate on the opposite color squares and attack the opponent's pawns.

The bishop cannot move or the knight would capture the c-pawn.

Black cannot retreat the king without allowing the white king to move to g5 winning the h-pawn.

The king is able to penetrate into black's territory along the dark squares.

The knight can also invade along the dark squares.

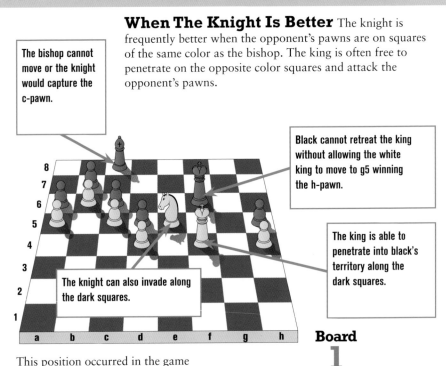

Board 1

This position occurred in the game Schlechter–Walbrodt, Vienna 1898.

Black cannot allow 2 ... b×c6 3 b7, when the pawn queens.

In the game, it was white's turn to move, and it won after some lengthy maneuvering. If it had been black's move, white would have won either by invading with the king after black's king moved, or by capturing the c-pawn after a bishop move: 1 ... ♗f5 2 ♘xc6.

Board 2

Two Bishops The two bishops have an advantage against a bishop and knight or two knights in most endings, especially when passed pawns are involved. The chief advantage is that it is usually easier for the owner of the two bishops to force favorable exchanges.

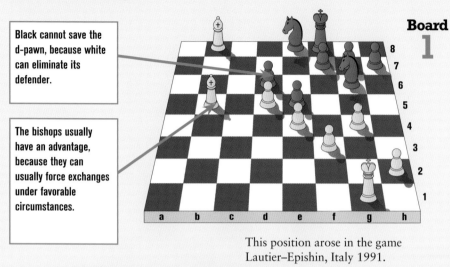

Black cannot save the d-pawn, because white can eliminate its defender.

The bishops usually have an advantage, because they can usually force exchanges under favorable circumstances.

Board 1

This position arose in the game Lautier–Epishin, Italy 1991.

The game continued: **1** ... f6 **2** ♗xe8 ♔xe8 **3** ♗xd6.

Trading pieces in order to arrive at a winning bishop versus knight ending is a constant theme in these endings.

Board 2

The Exchange

The capture of a piece or pawn while giving up material of equal value is called *exchanging*. When you capture a rook while giving up only a bishop or knight, you have won the exchange. The "exchange" is now shorthand for such a trade. A rook is much stronger in the endgame than either a bishop or a knight.

Rook Versus Bishop Without pawns the ending is normally drawn. The weaker side's king can go to either of the corners that are not accessible to the bishop.

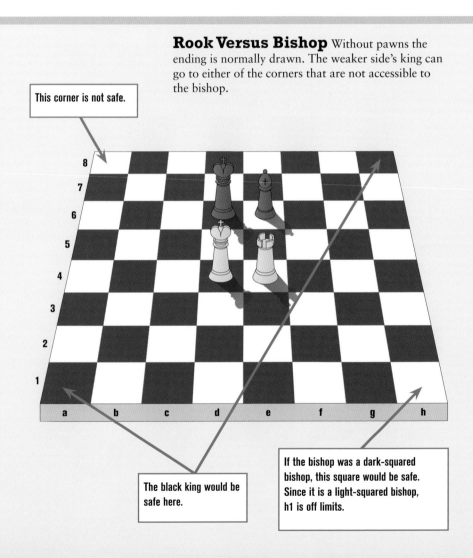

This corner is not safe.

The black king would be safe here.

If the bishop was a dark-squared bishop, this square would be safe. Since it is a light-squared bishop, h1 is off limits.

If the king is in the wrong corner, one winning idea is to threaten mate and the bishop simultaneously.

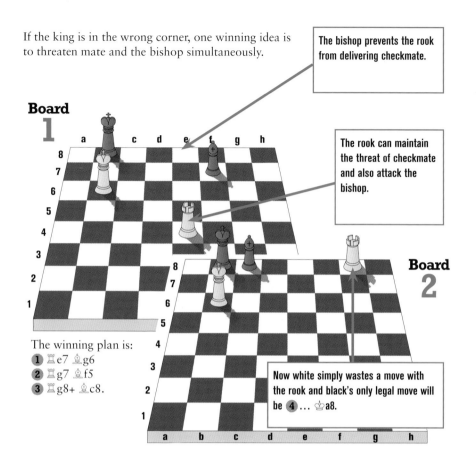

Board 1

The bishop prevents the rook from delivering checkmate.

The rook can maintain the threat of checkmate and also attack the bishop.

Board 2

The winning plan is:
1. ♖e7 ♗g6
2. ♖g7 ♗f5
3. ♖g8+ ♗c8.

Now white simply wastes a move with the rook and black's only legal move will be 4 ... ♔a8.

Board 3

White settles things with:
4. ♖h8.

The forced 4 ... ♔a8 is met by 5 ♖×c8#.

Rook Versus Bishop continued

A bishop and pawn can draw against a rook as long as they can protect one another and there is no immediate threat of mate.

> The bishop and pawn protect one another, and white cannot make any progress.

> White is in no danger either. Trading the rook for a pawn will leave black with insufficient mating material (king and bishop) and the game would be drawn.

Board 1

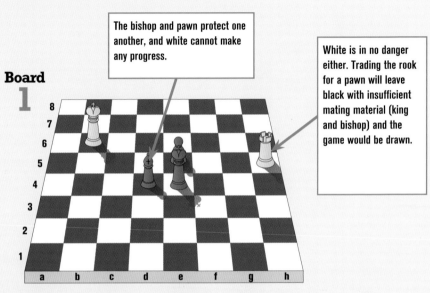

This is an ideal position for the defender.

Board 2

> A bishop plus two pawns will spell trouble for the rook. If they are connected passed pawns (☛ see p.179), the rook is virtually helpless.

With one more pawn, the bishop has a winning advantage.

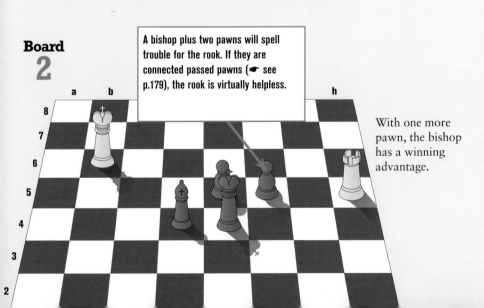

Rook Versus Knight

This ending is a draw if the knight is not cut off from the king, unless the defender is cornered.

The knight will be lost no matter where it moves.

Board 1

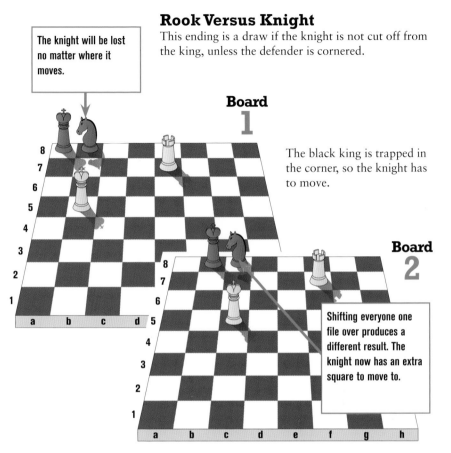

The black king is trapped in the corner, so the knight has to move.

Board 2

Shifting everyone one file over produces a different result. The knight now has an extra square to move to.

Here black has sufficient space in which to defend.

Black survives by playing:
1 ... ♘a7
2 ♔b6 ♘c8+.

Board 3

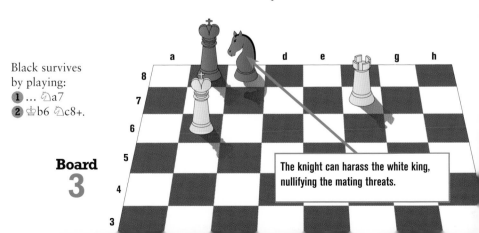

The knight can harass the white king, nullifying the mating threats.

Rook Versus Knight continued

The rook has better chances against a knight and two connected passed pawns than it does against the bishop in that situation.

Board 1

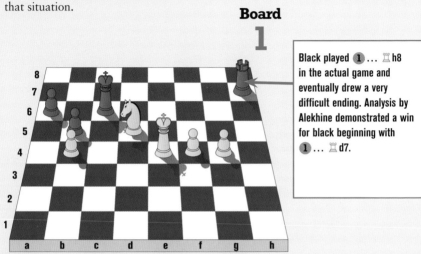

Black played **1** ... ♜h8 in the actual game and eventually drew a very difficult ending. Analysis by Alekhine demonstrated a win for black beginning with **1** ... ♜d7.

Here is a famous position from Emanuel Lasker–Edward Lasker, New York 1924.

The winning line begins:
1 ... ♜d7 **2** ♘e3 a5 **3** bxa5 b4.

Board 2

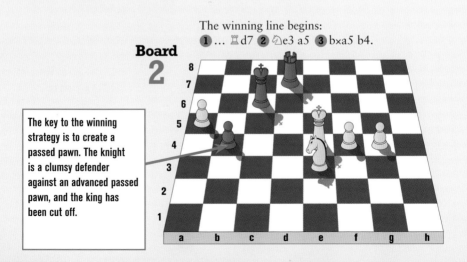

The key to the winning strategy is to create a passed pawn. The knight is a clumsy defender against an advanced passed pawn, and the king has been cut off.

White's pawns are not quite advanced enough to prevent black's winning maneuver.

Play continues: **4** g5 ♔c5 **5** ♘c2 b3 **6** ♘a3 b2 **7** g6 ♔b4.

The rook prevents the advance of the g-pawn and is ready to help the b-pawn advance.

The black king forces the knight to retreat.

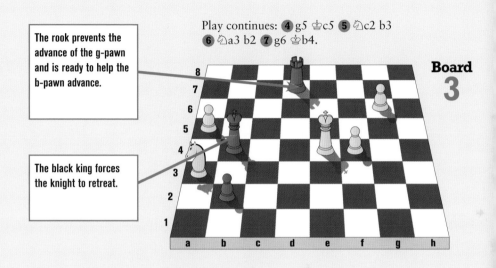

Board 3

Black seals the victory after **8** ♘b1 by playing: **8** ... ♖d1 **9** g7 ♖g1.

Board 4

The g-pawn is now lost and so is the game.

Mastery Challenges IX

☛ For answers, see pp.258 and 259

"Every pawn is a potential Queen."

James Mason (1849–1905)

1 **Essential pawn drill**
Demonstrate that you can draw as black. (Don't make it easy for yourself—play the best tries for white as well.)

Black to move

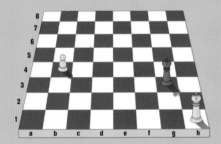

2 **Judge at a glance**
What's the result if it's white's move? What if it's black's?

3 **Nasty surprise**
Black to move and win.

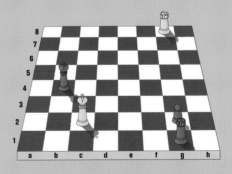

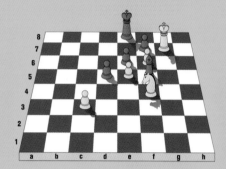

4 Zugzwang theme
White to move and win.

White to move

5 Win it for white
Find the quickest win.

6 Make a great save
White is two pawns down and would love a draw! Find it.

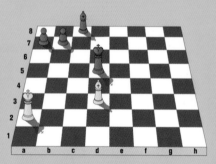

White to move

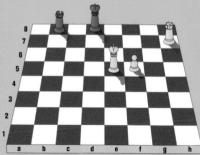

7 Make Philidor proud
Show how black can draw.

Black to move

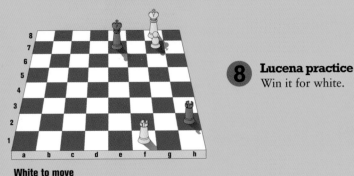

White to move

8 **Lucena practice**
Win it for white.

9 **Knight against pawn**
Can white draw?

White to move

ANSWERS

1 You should know this drawing procedure like an old friend. Black's first move is forced—it's the only move that draws: **1. ... Kd7!**. Black gets in front of the pawn and keeps the white king from c6. Now king moves by white clearly get him nowhere. So he tries advancing the pawn: **2. d6**. Now black has to make another exact move, but the technique is simple—be prepared to take the opposition: **2. ... Kd8! 3. Kc6 Kc8 4. d7+ Kd8 5. Kd6 stalemate.**

2 White to move promotes and wins. Black to move catches the pawn. The rule of the square (☞ see p.194) lets you see this right away.

3 1. ... Ra1!, and if white captures the pawn with 2. Rxg2, he'll lose his rook to the skewering 2. ... Ra2+!. If white doesn't capture the pawn, it will promote to a queen, guarded by the black rook.

4 1. Kg8! Bg4 (if 1. ... Be4, white will play 2. Nxe6!; then if 2. ... fxe6, the white pawn easily marches on to promotion) 2. Ng6! Bh5 3. Nh8!. Now black is in zugzwang and must give way with his king, allowing white to capture the f–pawn with his knight, when black's game crumbles.

5 1. Kb5! avoids stalemate and gains white two moves (tempo) toward the pawn. **1. ... Kb1** (or 1. ... Kb2) **2. Kc4+**, winning. Here's an interesting sample line: 2. ... Kc1 3. Qa7 Kb1 4. Kb3. Now if 4. ... a1(Q) 5. Qg1#. If 4. ... a1(N)+ (underpromotion), 5. Kc3 Nc2 6. Qh7! (pinning)!

6 1. Ba6!. If 1. ... bxa6, black would need to try to promote on a1, a dark square. But with a light-square bishop, black won't be able to force white's king out of the a1-corner. After 1. Ba6!, if black doesn't move his b–pawn, white will simply capture it. And if 1. ... b6, trying at least to keep a possible queen, white plays 2. Bxc8 and uses his extra bishop to draw easily against the two pawns.

7 1. ... Rb6! sets up Philidor's Defense, cutting off the white king. If 2. f6, black plays 2. ... Ke8!, toward the queening square: 3. Kf5 Rb1 4. Kg6 Rg1+. White can't make progress.

8 This is another key idea in the rook-and-pawn endings (☞ see p.219). 1. Re1+ Kd7 2. Re4!. White is planning on using his rook to shield his king from checks.

9 1. Ne1+!. When black's knight gets in front of the pawn, the knight can defend without the aid of his king.

How to Win a Chess Game

It's a challenge for beginners to know how to prioritize their thinking during a chess game. Playing chess can't, of course, be reduced to a formula or flowchart. But the steps below can definitely help when used with good judgment. After some practice, they become second nature.

If you combine the knowledge you've gained in this book with the methodology below, you'll win a lot of chess games! And when you study the game analyses in the next section, you'll see how the great players use the thought patterns below. Genius and creativity, however, sometimes make their own "rules."

In the opening, follow these three steps:

❶ Make one or two pawn moves that occupy or help control the center.
❷ Develop your pieces to squares that bear on the center.
❸ Castle to bring your king into safety and your rook toward the center.

When Considering Your Moves:
- Decide on one to three candidate moves that look good based on what you've learned about chess. Then analyze the consequences of each. (You'll see further and further ahead as you practice.)
- Before you make your chosen move, visualize it on the intended square. Make sure your piece on the new square is safe or guarded and can't be captured by an inferior piece—unless you intend a sacrifice.

How to Keep Improving

1. Practice with players who are about your level.
The "Chess on the Internet" section of this book (☛ see p.284) gives you online sites where you can find opponents. It also shows you where to find brick-and-mortar chess clubs.

2. Play over master games that explain their moves with words.
The next section of this book presents six world-famous games. Play over them repeatedly. You'll understand more every time you do. Find other master games that start with the openings you like and play over those, too.

3. Work chess puzzles.
You'll find them in newspapers, magazines, books, and online. Try to solve them before looking at the solution. Check your ideas against the answers and make sure you understand why the solution given works.

After the Opening—What to Think About

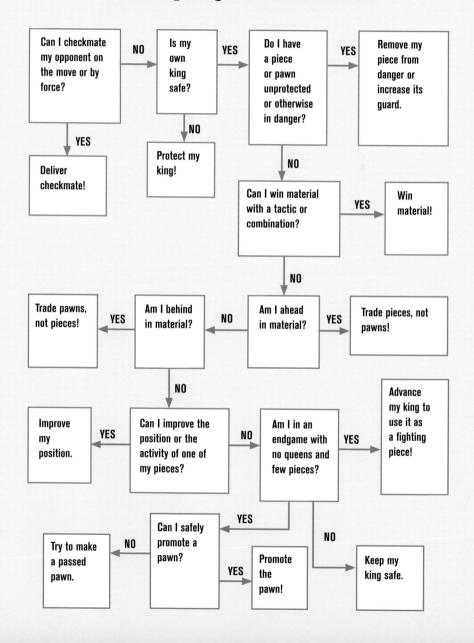

Section 10: BRINGING IT ALL TOGETHER WITH GAME ANALYSIS

You've learned the elements of chess more or less one by one. The best way to bring these ideas together to see how they perform in a real chess battle is to play over instructive games by the great masters—with some helpful explanations.

Set up a chessboard. Note that in books white always plays "up" the board, so set up your board as white from your perspective. Play over each move of a game thoughtfully. As you progress, verify the position on your board against the illustrations in the book. Replay these games often—you'll learn something every time you do.

Game 1: The Opera Box Game

Paul Morphy v. Karl, Duke of Brunswick & Count Isouard
Paris, 1858

We begin with perhaps the most famous game in the history of chess, a contest many expert players know by heart. Paul Morphy of New Orleans had completed his Doctorate of Law when he was too young to practice. While waiting for his 21st birthday, he toured Europe, defeating the world's top chess players. He was hailed as the unofficial world champion and lionized as a celebrity.

One night in Paris, two wealthy chess amateurs invited him to their private box at the opera. But once there, legend has it, they sat him with his back to the stage and insisted on his playing a game.

Paul Morphy's games changed how masters thought about chess.

Paul Morphy

1 e4 e5 2. Nf3 d6 3. d4

Look for the concepts of central control, development, initiative, and sacrifice.

Black's 2. ... d6 initiates the Philidor Defense, passive but solid. Black bolsters his central pawn on e5 while opening a diagonal for his light-square bishop. White keeps the initiative by attacking e5 again with 3. d4. If black plays 3. ... exd4, white's knight centralizes with 4. Nxd4.

3 ... Bg4

White threatened to win the e5–pawn with 4. dxe5 dxe5 5. Qxd8+ Kxd8 6. Nxe5. So black decides to *pin* (☞ see p.118) the knight to the queen. A better move would be to play 4. ... Nd7, guarding e5 while following the knights before bishops rule (☞ see p.43).

4 dxe5 Bxf3 5. Qxf3 dxe5 6. Bc4

White already threatens 7. Qxf7 checkmate! So black develops a piece while blocking the threat.

6 ... Nf6 7. Qb3!

White now attacks both f7 and b7. His control of the center permits him to shift his forces from one wing to the other.

7 ... Qe7 8. Nc3

8. Qxb7, winning a pawn, was another way. But Morphy, perhaps in a hurry to finish the game and turn his attention to the opera, is hunting for a quicker kill!

8 ... c6 9. Bg5

White pins the knight against the queen. Black is in a near *zugzwang* (☞ see p.193). His own queen blocks his bishop and is confined to lowly guard duty, watching over the b–pawn and the f–pawn.

Morphy's blue-blood opponents are understandably eager to push Morphy's bishop off c4, breaking up the *battery* attacking f7—generally the weakest point in black's camp until he castles.

9 ... b5

10 Nxb5!

Morphy sacrifices his knight to keep the attack going.

10 ... cxb5 11. Bxb5+ Nbd7
12. 0–0–0 Rd8

Morphy now sacrifices a rook-for-knight *exchange* (☞ see p.250) to add fuel to black's funeral pyre. 13. Bxd7 would not be as good. Morphy wants to maintain the pin along the a4–e8 diagonal.

13 Rxd7 Rxd7 14. Rd1

Morphy's last piece joins the king-hunt. Black may be up a rook, but all his pieces are either tied down or asleep at home.

14 ...Qe6 15. Bxd7+ Nxd7

Perhaps black thought he was finally safe, about to bring out his bishop and to castle, making his extra piece count. But Morphy unveils a final and lethal surprise—a queen sacrifice (☞ see p.131).

16 Qb8+ Nxb8 17. Rd8#

Like the jaw-dropping ending to a good movie thriller, this game's denouement is both surprising and logical.

Game 2: The Evergreen Game

Adolf Anderssen v. Jean Dufresne
Berlin, 1852

German Adolf Anderssen was recognized as the best player in the world until the rise of Paul Morphy. When Morphy quickly retired from chess, Anderssen was again number one. His opponent in this game, Jean Dufresne, was a leading chess author and chess master.

One of the greatest games in chess lore, even modern world champions are enchanted by Anderssen's play in the so-called *Evergreen Game*. Look for the concepts of gambit, initiative, and discovered double check.

Adolf Anderssen postage stamp

① e4 e5 2. Nf3 Nc6 3. Bc4 Bc5

Each player has staked out the center with one pawn move and developed a knight and then a bishop—very sensible classical play.

④ b4

The Evans Gambit: White offers a pawn to gain the initiative.

④ ... Bxb4 5. c3 Ba5 6. d4 exd4 7. 0–0 d3 8. Qb3

White creates a *battery* to attack f7, the pre-castling weak point in black's camp in the king–pawn openings. Black is on the defensive.

⑧ ... Qf6 9. e5

⑨ ... Qg6

Black can't safely capture white's e5-pawn. After 9. ... Nxe5, 10. Re1 (pinning!) d6 11. Nxe5 dxe5 12. Qa4+ Bd7 13. Qxa5, winning a piece, would be one way to punish black.

⑩ Re1

A computer evaluation shows this position as equal overall. But that means white has an initiative worth the two pawns black is materially ahead.

⑩ ... Nge7 11. Ba3 b5

Black decides to give back some material, intending to take the pressure off f7 and develop some initiative of his own. Castling (11. ... 0–0) is also appealing and would get his king out of the center.

⑫ Qxb5 Rb8 13. Qa4 Bb6 14. Nbd2 Bb7

Again, black prefers to get his own counterattack going rather than castle. (It was the "romantic" era in chess!)

⑮ Ne4 Qf5?! 16. Bxd3 Qh5 17. Nf6+

17 gxf6 18. exf6 Rg8!

Black uses the newly opened g–file to counterattack immediately. He threatens 19. ... Qxf3! and 20. ... Qxg2#.

19 Rad1!

Anderssen sees black's plan and prepares a diabolical response.

19 ... Qxf3

A tempting move, especially to someone who has been under fire the whole game and sees his chance to threaten checkmate. But 19. ... Qh3 would have been better, keeping the game about even. Now white launches an unstoppable sacrificial onslaught.

20 Rxe7+!! Nxe7

White wins whatever black choses. One pretty example: 20. ... Kd8 21. Rxd7+! Kc8 22. Rd8+ Nxd8 23. Qd7+ Kxd7 24. Bf5+ and 25. Bd7#.

21 Qxd7+!! Kxd7 22. Bf5++

Discovered double check!

22 ... Ke8 23. Bd7+ Kf8 24. Bxe7#

Black played some good moves but missed the poison contained in white's 19. Rd1!. But who can blame Dufresne? Anderssen concocted one of the most beautiful checkmating combinations of all time, immortalizing both players.

Game 3: Rubinstein's Immortal Game

George Rotlewi v. Akiba Rubinstein
Lodz, Poland, 1907

Polish master Akiba Rubinstein was perhaps the strongest player never to be world champion. In this game, he's matched against another accomplished Polish master. Although most of us will never play a combination as brilliant as Rubinstein's, we could have prevented it with the ideas already learned in this book.

This game, another that has been replayed by countless chess aficionados for more than a hundred years, is a marvel of imagination and clear-minded calculation. First play over the main moves and read the explanations. Leave the alternative variations for a second look. This is good advice in general when playing over master games.

Akiba Rubinstein

① d4 d5 2. Nf3 e6 3. e3 c5 4. c4

With his last move, white transposes into a variation of the Queen's Gambit Declined called the *Tarrasch Defense*.

④ ... Nc6 5. Nc3 Nf6 6. dxc5

As we've learned, white could maintain the tension in the center by not exchanging central pawns. A good alternative is 6. Bd3.

⑥ ... Bxc5 7. a3 a6 8. b4 Bd6
9. Bb2 0–0 10. Qd2

After 10. cxd5, black would have the isolated queen's pawn (☞ see p.169). White can't safely win a pawn: After 10. cxd5 exd5 11. Nxd5 Nxd5 12. Qxd5?, black would win the white

queen with the discovered attack 12. ... Bxb4+!

⑩ ... Qe7

Black offers a pawn sacrifice to take over the initiative: If 11. cxd5 exd5 12. Nxd5 Nxd5 13. Qxd5 Rd8!, threatening 14. ... Bxb4+, another discovered attack on white's queen.

11 Bd3 dxc4 12. Bxc4 b5 13. Bd3 Rd8
14. Qe2

White gets his queen off the d–file.

14 ... Bb7 15. 0–0 Ne5 16. Nxe5 Bxe5

Black threatens a combination:
17. ... Bxh2+ 18. Kxh2 Qd6+, using a
double attack to win white's bishop on d3
and come out a pawn ahead.

17 f4

White blocks the h2–b8 diagonal to stop
the threatened combination. But 17. Rfd1
was better, putting a rook on the open
file—as you've learned to do. The move
would protect the bishop—without
weakening the pawn structure in front
of white's king.

17 ... Bc7 18. e4

This opens the g1–a7 diagonal to white's
king. Once again, bringing a rook to an
open file would be better: 18. Rac1!.

18 ... Rac8 19. e5?

> A serious mistake. Rotlewi lacks a
> sense of danger to his king, now wide
> open to diagonal attacks from both
> black's long-range bishops.

Again, bringing a rook to the open file was
better, this time with 19. Rad1.

19 ... Bb6+ 20. Kh1

20 ... Ng4!

> This is not a one-piece attack. All
> of black's pieces are deployed for
> the assault.

21 Be4

White tries to block the deadly long
diagonal to his king. But it's too late.
His careless play has left his king too
vulnerable. One hundred years of analysis
has shown white has no effective defense.

A few example lines: If 21. Bxh7+, then ... Kxh7 22. Qxg4 Rd2! highlights the fatal weakness on g2. Or 21. h3 Qh4 22. Qxg4 Qxg4 23. hxg4 Rxd3, threatening both ... Rh3 mate and ... Rxc3. Or if the straightforward 21. Qxg4, then ... Rxd3 leaves white lost in all lines. But don't worry about seeing all this. The actual game shows the most beautiful variation.

㉑ ... Qh4 22. g3

Or 22. h3 Rxc3! 23. Bxc3 Bxe4 24. Qxg4 Qxg4 25. hxg4 Rd3, with the threat of ... Rh3# is another splendid demolition Rubinstein had to foresee.

㉒ ... Rxc3!! 23. gxh4

White accepts black's queen sacrifice. If white instead tries 23. Bxb7, then ... Rxg3! 24. Bd4 Nxh2 25. Qxh2 Rh3 provides another deadly pin.

㉓ ... Rd2!!

㉔ Qxd2 Bxe4+ 25. Qg2 Rh3!, white resigns.

White doesn't want to see his king checkmated. There are no saving moves: 26. Rf3 Bxf3 27. Bd4 Bxd4 28. Rf1 Rxh2#, or: 26. Rf2 (to block the killing dark-square diagonal) ... Bxf2 27. Qxe4 Rxh2#:

| What a picture postcard from Chess Funland! White's king is caught in the corner without cover, checkmated by a team of impudent ruffians while his still-mighty army looks on. | Notice that if it were white's move, his queen could checkmate black with Qa8. But the first checkmate ends the game! |

Game 4: Capablanca's Deflection

Ossip Bernstein v. José Raúl Capablanca, Moscow, 1914

Some consider José Capablanca the greatest player of all time. When he played this game, he was not yet world champion—that would wait until 1921. But the handsome young Cuban was already considered one of the top two or three players in the world at the time of this game. Bernstein, a brilliant Russian attorney, was in the top ten. The game was a tense, equal struggle between titans until the very last move. Look for the concepts of hanging pawns and back-rank weakness.

José Raúl Capablanca

1. d4 d5 2. c4 e6 3. Nc3 Nf6 4. Nf3 Be7 5. Bg5 0–0 6. e3 Nbd7 7. Rc1 b6

Black's light-square bishop is his problem piece to develop in the Queen's Gambit Declined.

8. cxd5 exd5 9. Qa4

> "Capa" plans to use a queenside fianchetto to get his bishop into the game.

White waits to develop his light-square bishop because he has a plan to trade it.

9. ... Bb7 10. Ba6

White plays to swap his bishop for black's fianchettoed bishop. Black has put his queenside pawns on dark squares. So his bishop would have been the main protector of the light squares.

10 ... Bxa6 11. Qxa6 c5 12. Bxf6

12. 0–0 would be another solid choice—and less committal.

12 ... Nxf6 13. dxc5 bxc5

Notice that black has *hanging pawns* (☛ see pp.185 and 186). These pawns can be both an asset, because they control lots of important squares, and a target, because they require protection from friendly pieces. The game is dynamically equal. Each side has offsetting strengths and weaknesses, which makes for an exciting game.

14 0–0 Qb6 15. Qe2

White wants to keep knockout power on the board. So he avoids the exchange of queens.

15 ... c4

This was a novel idea at the time, a seeming violation of classical principles. Black leaves a "hole" on d4 for a white knight and makes his own d–pawn *backward*. But he pushes for the initiative on the queenside.

16 Rfd1 Rfd8 17. Nd4

White's knight takes up a central position while blockading black's d–pawn.

17 ... Bb4

Black judges that white's knight on c3, which attacks black's d–pawn, is more valuable in this position than the bishop. A master knows that the value of the pieces fluctuates depending on the position.

18 b3

White wants to break up black's central pawn duo and open lines for his rooks. But instead, 18. h3 has its merits, providing *luft* for his king (☛ see p.148).

18 ... Rac8 19. bxc4 dxc4

Now the argument revolves around black's passed pawn. White has blockaded it, and the game is still equal, but a fight.

20 Rc2 Bxc3 21. Rxc3 Nd5

Capablanca's knight takes up an influential post, controlling c3 in front of black's passed pawn.

㉒ Rc2 c3

After 22. ... Nf4, 23. exf4, black regains his piece with 23. ... Rxd4 24. Rxd4 Qxd4, when white would have a doubled f–pawn. But the game would still be approximately equal. Capablanca is still fishing for more.

㉓ Rdc1

White doubles his rooks against the passed pawn. But the rooks don't have much scope.

㉓ ... Rc5 24. Nb3 Rc6 25. Nd4

> White may be suggesting a draw by repetition of moves. Black declines!

㉕ ... Rc7 26. Nb5

White could have avoided what's to come with 26. h3, making an escape square for his king.

㉖ ... Rc5

It appears that white can win the c–pawn, because he attacks it three times and it's defended only twice. Is it a key capture, or is it bait in a trap?

㉗ Nxc3?

㉗ ... Nxc3 28. Rxc3 Rxc3 29. Rxc3

㉙ ... Qb2!!, white resigns.

> After this thunderbolt, Bernstein resigns! Do you see why? If 30. Qxb2, black plays 30. ... Rd1#!

Capablanca has played a wonderful deflection combination (☛ see p.132). White has no saving move. If he defends against checkmate, he loses his rook. Note that if 30. Qd3, black would not capture the queen with 30. ... Rxd3 because of 31. Rc8+ and white would actually checkmate black on the next move. Instead, after 30. Qd3, black would continue 30. ... Qa1+ 31. Qf1 Qxc3, leaving Capablanca a rook ahead— hopeless for white.

Game 5: Fischer's Shutout

Robert Fischer v. Pal Benko
New York, 1963

American Bobby Fischer is still the best-known chess player in the world. He's most famous for dethroning the old Soviet Union's Boris Spassky in 1972 in a Cold War chess showdown. The young American ended two decades of Soviet domination of the World Chess Championship. Then Fischer never again played an official game of chess.

One of Fischer's unique achievements was his 11–0 sweep in the 1963–64 U.S. Championship. This shutout remains a record in major national championships. His opponent in the game featured below, Pal Benko, was a Hungarian who defected to the U.S. in 1957 to escape Soviet rule. He was a World Championship candidate more than once—and in his prime in 1963.

This game was the next-to-last round in the famous 11–0 shutout. Fischer's opponents were trying hard to stop his winning streak, because he had perturbed them by announcing he would win 11–0. Some of Benko's first 16 moves have, over the years, sometimes been criticized. But his moves were quite strong. He made only one serious mistake, but one that allowed his opponent a startling rook sacrifice.

> The opening is the Pirc Defense, a hypermodern challenge to white's classical center (☛ see p.111). Fischer generally followed very classical principles, here setting up a broad pawn center. So these early moves already prepare us for a battle of chess ideas.

Bobby Fischer

❶ e4 g6 2. d4 Bg7 3. Nc3 d6 4. f4 Nf6 5. Nf3 0–0 6. Bd3 Bg4 7. h3

Black pinned white's knight on f3, weakening the defenses of the white pawn on d4. But after 7. h3, black must capture, trading his bishop for the knight. Retreating with 7. ... Bh5 would lose the bishop to 8. g4.

7 ... Bxf3
8. Qxf3 Nc6

Black develops his knight with a tempo against white's now-undefended d–pawn. White defends it by developing his bishop.

9 Be3 e5

This is a very good move. It's time for black to make his own thrust in the center to try to dissolve white's dominance there.

10 dxe5 dxe5 **11.** f5

Fischer also makes the best move, pushing past e5 to attack the kingside. The game is roughly equal, but black has to find the best defensive plan.

11 ... gxf5 **12.** Qxf5 Nd4 **13.** Qf2

13. Qxe5 is possible, but after 13. ... Ng4! (discovering an attack on white's queen) 14. Qg5 Nxe3 15. Qxe3 Qh4+ 16. g3 Qh5, white's attack has stalled.

13 ... Ne8

Black wants to unblock his bishop and relocate his knight.

14 0–0 Nd6

This is the defensive setup Benko envisioned. Black started the game without occupying the center but now is entrenched in the middle of the board.

15 Qg3 Kh8

Black unpins his bishop.

16 Qg4!

Fischer prevents 16. ... f5 and gives his queen access to h5.

16 ... c6

Black prevents Nd5.

17 Qh5

17 ... Qe8?

Benko's only real blunder. But Fischer needs only one. Black could have shored up his defenses with 17. ... Ne6.

18 Bxd4 exd4 19. Rf6!!

We can better understand Benko's mistake by seeing that, if Fischer had tried the natural 19. e5, black would have played 19. ... f5, uncovering an attack on white's queen. After 20. Qxe8 Nxe8, Benko would have achieved a completely equal position! But after 19. Rf6!!, black is lost.

19 ... Kg8

If 19. ... Bxf6 or 19. ... exf3, white has 20. e5!, and there's no escape from the straightforward mate on h7. And if 19. ... h6, 20. e5! is again a winner:
20. ... dxc3
21. Rxh6+ Bxh6
22. Qxh6+ Kg8
23. Qh7#.

Fischer sacrifices a whole rook to block black's f-pawn from advancing to f5, where it would block the d3–h7 diagonal.

20 e5 h6 21. Ne2

Black resigns!

If black doesn't move the knight, white will capture it and be ahead a whole piece, a hopeless situation against another master.

If 21. ... Bxf6, 22. Qxh6 will lead to checkmate.

Black's knight on d6 is marked for extinction. If black moves the knight, white plays Qf5, lining up an unstoppable battery to checkmate on h7.

Game 6: Carlsen Gives Notice

Magnus Carlsen v. Sipke Ernst
Wijk aan Zee, Holland, 2004

Magnus Carlsen of Norway became the Chess World Champion in 2013 at 22 years old. When he was 13 and relatively unknown, he put the world on notice by a sensational performance that earned him his first step toward the international grandmaster title. In the next-to-last round, he was tied with his chief rival, another promising young teen from Holland. Carlsen defeated him in the blaze of tactics below, which earned the Norwegian teen a "Spectators' Prize." Look for the concepts of central control, opposite-side castling, and rook lift.

Magnus Carlsen

① e4 c6 2. d4 d5

As you've learned, in the Caro-Kann Defense, black supports his pawn on d5 with one on c6, without hemming in his light-squared bishop.

③ Nc3 dxe4 4. Nxe4 Bf5 5. Ng3 Bg6 6. h4

Black must immediately make a getaway square for his bishop. With best play, the line is equal. But the play is razor sharp.

⑥ ... h6

6. ... h5 would weaken black's kingside pawn structure even more.

⑦ Nf3 Nd7 8. h5 Bh7 9. Bd3 Bxd3 10. Qxd3

White has used his first-move initiative to weaken the black kingside and allow himself the possibility of using the h–file for his rook.

White puts his knight on a commanding square, from which it can leap into the attack.

16 ... Rad8 17. Qe2 c5 18. Ng6!

An imaginative move—and the best one in the position.

10 ... e6 11. Bf4 Ngf6 12. 0–0–0

White continues to play aggressively. He plans an attack on the kingside, so he tucks his king away on the queenside and connects his rooks.

18 ... fxg6

Black should resist taking the knight sacrifice and instead play 18. ... Rfe8 19. Nxe7+ Rxe7 20. dxc5 Red7 21. Rxd7 Rxd7 22. Be3, when white is a pawn up but only slightly better.

12 ... Be7 13. Ne4 Qa5 14. Kb1 0–0 15. Nxf6+ Nxf6 16. Ne5

19 Qxe6+ Kh8 20. hxg6 Ng8

Black overlooks another sacrifice, but even after the superior 20. ... Qb6, white has a winning advantage after 21. Qxe7 Ng8 22. Qe4 cxd4 23. Be5.

21 **Bxh6! gxh6 22. Rxh6+ Nxh6 23. Qxe7**

White threatens 24. Qh7#.

23 **... Nf7 24. gxf7 Kg7**

There is no adequate defense. For example, after 24. ... Qb6 25. Qe5+ Kh7 26. Rh1+ Kg6 27. Rh5 Qf6, white has the deflection sacrifice (☞ see p.132). 28. Rh6+, winning the black queen.

25 **Rd3 Rd6 26. Rg3+ Rg6**

Between white's queen and rook, black's king is in too much of a crossfire. Black brings his own rook up to try to block the attacks.

27 **Qe5+ Kxf7 28. Qf5+ Rf6 29. Qd7#**

White is straightjacketed by his own rooks.

A beautiful variation on the epaulette mate.

GLOSSARY

Active (i) A description of a move that increases a player's mobility; (ii) a description of a piece that is mobile.

Annotation An explanation of a chess move or an examination of alternatives.

Back rank A player's own first rank.

Back rank mate A checkmate delivered by a rook or queen on an opponent's first rank, when the king is trapped behind pawns.

Backward pawn A trailing pawn that has no pawn protection of its own.

Bad bishop A bishop whose mobility is restricted by its own pawns.

Blockade A situation where one side cannot advance, usually used in terms of preventing the advance of a passed pawn.

Blunder A poor move with serious drawbacks.

Capture Taking an opponent's piece with one of your own.

Castling A move involving both the king and a rook.

Center The squares d4, d5, e4, and e5.

Centralization The act of bringing pieces to influence the center.

Check An attack on the king.

Checkmate When the king is in check and cannot escape the attack.

Closed game A game where piece movement is restricted by interlocking pawns.

Combination A series of forced moves leading to an advantage.

Decoy sacrifice A sacrifice that entices the opponent to move a piece to a less favorable location.

Development The movement of pieces off their original squares.

Diagonal Any contiguous line of squares along which a bishop can move.

Diagram A drawing of a chess position.

Discovered attack The movement of a piece that results in an attack from a piece that did not move.

Discovered check The movement of a piece that results in a check from a piece that did not move.

Double attack A simultaneous attack on two enemy pieces by a single piece or pawn.

Double check A discovered check when the moving piece also delivers a check.

Doubled pawns Two pawns of the same color on the same file.

Draw A completed chess game without a winner.

Edge The outside squares of the board.

En passant French for "in passing."

Endgame Also called the *ending*. The third and last phase of the game, following a significant reduction of material.

Equalize To achieve a balanced position.

Escape square A square to which a checked king can move.

Exchange (i) The trading of equal amounts of material; (ii) the capture of a rook by a bishop or knight.

Fianchetto The placement of a bishop on b2 and/or g2 as white, or on b7 and/or g7 as black.

FIDE The acronym for the International Chess Federation (Fédération Internationale des Échecs).

File Any of the eight columns on a chessboard.

Flank Sometimes called the *wing*. Refers to one or other side of the board.

Flank openings A set of openings in which white does not make an early advance of the d- or e-pawns.

Fork An attack on two enemy chessmen at the same time.

Gambit Any opening featuring a planned sacrifice.

Grandmaster The highest title awarded by FIDE.

Half-open file A file on which only one side has a pawn.

Hanging pawns Two adjacent pawns that are on the 4th rank, unsupported by other pawns and on half-open files.

Hole The square directly in front of a backward pawn.

Initiative The term used to describe the advantage held by the player dictating play.

Interposition The movement of a piece between a piece that is attacked and its attacker.

Isolated pawn A pawn whose adjacent files contain no other pawn of the same color.

Kingside The e-, f-, g-, and h-files.

Lever A term for a white and black pawn diagonally adjacent so that either may capture the other.

Luft German for "air," a flight square for the king.

Majority A numerical superiority of pawns on one flank or the other.

Middlegame The phase of the game after the opening and before the ending.

Minority attack The advance of one or more pawns on a flank where the opponent has a majority of pawns.

Mobility The ability to move one's pieces about the board freely.

Notation A means of recording a chess game.

Open file A file that has no pawns.

Open game A set of openings characterized by active piece play.

Opening The beginning part of a chess game when the objective is the development of the pieces.

Opposition When only one square separates the kings on a rank, file, or diagonal.

Outpost A piece in the opponent's territory supported by a pawn and unable to be driven off by an enemy pawn.

Overload A situation in which one piece cannot do all that is asked of it.

Passed pawn A pawn with no enemy pawn hindering its advance.

Passive (i) Description of a move that contains no threats; (ii) description of a piece with limited mobility.

Pawn chain A diagonal set of pawns protecting one another.

Perpetual check A situation in which the king cannot free itself from an endless series of checks. The game is declared a draw.

Pin A tactic that immobilizes one piece or pawn.

Promotion When a pawn reaches the 8th rank, it must be exchanged for a piece, usually the queen.

Queenside The a-, b-, c-, and d-files.

Rank Any horizontal row on the chessboard.

Sacrifice To deliberately give up material.

Skewer An attack on a piece that results in a win of a less valuable piece.

Smothered mate A checked king that cannot move because all surrounding squares are occupied.

Stalemate One side cannot make any legal move, but is not in check. The result is a draw.

Strategy The long-range plan.

Tactics A move or set of moves that produces a short-term advantage.

Tempo Latin for "time." To lose a tempo is equivalent to losing a turn.

Zugzwang A condition in which a player must move, but any move would weaken the position.

KEY

A quick reference guide to the diagrams
and chess notation used in this book.

CHESS ON THE INTERNET

Listed here are some of the best-known chess sites on the Internet. The Internet changes rapidly, of course, but these sites have been around for a while.

Places to Play

www.chess.com
Play others from all over the world and get an online rating, for free. You'll automatically play against opponents close to your own rating. Because this service is web-based, working within your browser, you don't need to download any programs. Pay a monthly fee to add high-quality instructional materials, including videos and chess quizzes.

www.chessclub.com
The Internet Chess Club. Enjoy a free trial membership, but after it expires, you need to buy one. To use ICC, download software from its site.

www.freechess.org
One of the oldest free sites dedicated to chess. It also requires a software download.

www.chesskid.com
A kids-oriented site by the same crew that serves up chess.com.

Chess Organizations

www.uschess.org
The home of the United States Chess Federation, offering free news and information. Find clubs and official tournaments by state. If you join, you receive a monthly magazine as well as other benefits. You can buy chess books, videos, and official equipment.

www.fide.com
The home of the International Chess Federation. Find information on the world's top players and nearly 160 member countries.

Other Sites of Interest

https://saintlouischessclub.org
The site of one of the most active chess clubs in the U.S. and the sponsors of the annual U.S. Chess Championship, as well as other world-class events. Watch live action, for free, with instructive and entertaining commentary.

www.chessbase.com
International news from around the world. Chessbase is famous for its electronic databases (millions of games!) and the software to manage them.

www.theweekinchess.com
Chess news and games from around the world, along with book reviews and a calendar of world chess.

www.chessdom.com
www.chessbomb.com
Watch major tournaments live.

http://analyse.deep-chess.de
Analyze your game (or any game) with a selection of powerful chess "engines" that evaluate the position move by move. You can also set up and solve chess problems.

www.chessgames.com
Find famous master games and play them out on an online board—for free.

READING LIST

Many books were consulted while working on this book. The most significant sources were:

Alburt, Lev. *Chess Training Pocket Book*. Chess Information Research Center. 2000

Alburt, Lev and Krogius, Nikolai. *Just the Facts!* Chess Information Research Center. 2000

Burgess, Graham. *The Mammoth Book of Chess*. Robinson. 1997

de Firmian, Nick. *Modern Chess Openings*. McKay. 1999

Hooper and Whyld, *The Oxford Companion to Chess*, 2nd Edition. Oxford University Press. 1992

Pachman, Ludek and Russell, A. S. *Modern Chess Strategy*. Dover. 1963

Silman, Jeremy. *The Complete Book of Chess Strategy*. Siles Press. 1998

Soltis, Andrew. *Pawn Structure Chess*. McKay. 1976

Watson, John. *Secrets of Modern Chess Strategy*. Gambit. 1998

Suggestions for Additional Reading

If you only want a single volume reference on chess, then either *Chess for Dummies* or *The Complete Idiot's Guide to Chess* should serve your purposes. If you are willing to invest a little more time and money, then I recommend Grandmaster Lev Alburt's *Comprehensive Chess Course*. Alburt is a three-time U.S. Chess Champion. The first two volumes are designed to get you up and running as a chess player. The next five volumes are intended to make you a tournament caliber player.

Comprehensive Chess Course Volumes 1 and 2 are co-authored by Alburt and Roman Pelts. Volumes 3–5 are co-authored by Alburt and Sam Palatnik and are entitled *Chess Tactics*, *The King in Jeopardy*, and *Chess Strategy*. Volume 6 is by Alburt alone and is called *Chess Training Pocket Book*. Volume 7 is called *Just the Facts* and was co-authored by Alburt and Nikolai Krogius. Al Lawrence is the executive editor of the series.

These excellent books are available at www.chesswithlev.com, or write to Grandmaster Lev Alburt at P.O. Box 534, Gracie Square Station, New York, N.Y. 10028.

Another can't-miss author is Jeremy Silman. I was very impressed by his *The Complete Book of Chess Strategy*. When asking for recommendations, I've often heard the same phrase: "Anything by Silman."

INDEX